What Do Children Dream?

What Do Children Dream?

Gérard Bléandonu

Translated by
Sophie Leighton

FREE ASSOCIATION BOOKS

First published in 2006 by
FREE ASSOCIATION BOOKS
57 Warren Street
London W1T 5NR

www.fabooks.com

Originally published in 2002 as *Á quoirêvent nos enfants?*

A CIP catalogue record for this book is available
from the British Library.

ISBN 1 85343 729 8 pbk

Designed and produced for the publisher by
Chase Publishing Services Ltd, Sidmouth, EX10 9QG
Printed and bound in the European Union by
CPI Antony Rowe, Eastbourne, England

Contents

Introduction

When we open a book for the first time, we are generally anticipating a pleasant or interesting surprise. What might we read about dreams that would fall into this category? A dream is a fleeting moment that can never be recaptured or mechanically recorded and that only sometimes lingers in the memory. The dream is also a chaotic production that can be transformed into a fiction that expresses a truth.

It seems probable that dreams date back to the dawn of humanity. Two questions have been posed: first, what is the connection between dreams and the realm of consciousness, or reality? Second, how are they to be interpreted? From a very early stage, there have been those who have specialised in the social processing of dream phenomena. This specialisation still exists in traditional societies and at the margins of modern societies. Dreams have been studied by anthropologists, sociologists, psychoanalysts and historians, as well as by psychologists and neurophysiologists.

A review of the current state of knowledge is one possible approach to the subject but this would not explain the enigma as to the underlying nature of dreams. This book is not an attempt to remove the mystery. My sole purpose here is to consider children's dreams. This poses a challenge because, although all major libraries and bookshops have sections for books about dreams, the number of books devoted to children's dreams can be counted on one hand. As very commonly occurs, the study of dreams in children started with the application of what had already been discovered about adults.

The main difficulty is that children may not have the mental capacity to produce a dream narrative, less still any desire to remember it. In a comment that closely reflects everyday experience, a paediatrician with extensive knowledge concerning children's sleep observed: 'When I started writing this book on children's sleep, I thought that the chapter on dreams would be very straightforward and that applying everything I had learnt from books on the subject to clinical work would be a simple matter. Feeling interested and curious, I put some questions to the young patients who came to see me and were old enough to speak and ... silence ... followed by a shy remark, "I don't have dreams", which brought the questioning to an end. I was most disappointed, having looked forward to a nice collection of children's dreams!'[1]

When I began to write this book I had already collected a substantial number of children's dreams, which I had recorded during my clinical work with children suffering from psychological difficulties. In the course of my medical studies, followed by training in adult psychiatry, I had obtained many forms of knowledge about dreams. However, I have given precedence here to psychoanalytic theory because I use it in my clinical practice and because it seems to me to provide the best linchpin for all the relevant subject areas.

It would have been possible to write my book exclusively with reference to psychoanalysis. Dreams would then have been interpreted purely in terms of the relational context of the transference. The dream report would have been addressed to someone or been stated to have been dreamt in order to be addressed to someone. However, since the 1950s, sleep has become a subject of scientific study. Scientists have found that dream reports can often be obtained by waking an experimental subject during REM (rapid-eye-movement) sleep, or paradoxical sleep. Dreams have been studied in an objective way that takes account of the relational context. The interest in the process has eclipsed any concern with interpretation of the content.

My study of children's dreams is based on some fundamental principles. The scientific approach provides a method of investigating dream processes but not the meaning of their content. There is an essential distinction between the dream as a psychological phenomenon and paradoxical sleep as a biological process, although the former may have been based on the latter before developing in its own right. Freud's theory of dreams as a form of wish-fulfilment (or guardian of sleep) no longer seems adequate.

It has been observed that while Euclidean geometry has a very direct application to everyday life, investigating the universe requires recourse to non-Euclidean forms of geometry. Similarly, classical psychoanalytic dream theory is well suited to the analysis of neurotic adults. However, therapies conducted with individuals suffering from psychotic, psychosomatic, narcissistic, borderline or post-traumatic disorders provide a better basis for comparison and debate with scientific findings and hypotheses.

The dream work constitutes an integral part of mental processing. Children's dreams provide further confirmation of the cognitive contribution of the dream. Although this experience is obtained in an 'autistic' way, it gains its psychological value in a relationship with an adult. The child's dream develops in close connection with what I term the 'maternal reverie', which I will be discussing in more detail later. Unlike adults' dreams, which can form a discrete subject of study, children's dreams are part of the entire developmental process. The therapeutic approach to these is connected with the approach to play. Dreams and play complement each other in fostering the development of the personality. They combine emotional, affective and cognitive aspects.

Dreams can be distinguished according to the age and personality organisation of the dreamer. Nightmares merit separate discussion because of their frequency and their impact, which are often underestimated. These bear similarities with post-traumatic dreams, the study of which is informing our general understanding of dreams. Some people have asked if post-traumatic dreams may in fact be the rule rather than the exception in children. There is some evidence for this viewpoint from the way in which congenitally blind children manage to develop a dream life.

Adults' dreams will also be discussed in this book: these form an essential point of comparison because sleep and dreams in adults represent the culmination of gradual changes that extend from the foetal stage to adolescence.

Finally, I shall examine the functions of paradoxical sleep and dreams. In childhood, sleep and dreams influence the constitution of the inner life and its regulatory processes. The production of dream material and the narration of oneiric experiences play a significant role in this period of life.

Part One
What is the Function
of Children's Dreams?

1
Young Children's Dreams

One obvious fact applies to every dreamer: only he has direct access to the experience that has occurred during sleep. Dreams can be communicated only in narrative form. *Children become interesting as dreamers once they are capable of speaking, relating the experience they have had and imparting it to other people.* Accordingly, psychoanalysis developed a dream theory based on the childhood memories of adults. When children themselves were then listened to, older children were selected.

There has been a tendency to seek the key to childhood not where it may have been lost but where adult narratives have shed light on it. Some progress was made when some writers reported observations of their own children or children with whose family situations and lives they were very familiar. They then extrapolated their findings to children in general.

With the expansion of psychoanalysis, it was observed that young children rarely told their dreams spontaneously. The analyst has to help young children to discover and tell their dreams. He often has to draw on his own psychic reserves to enable the infant to communicate a dream narrative. The analyst therefore magnifies his interpretation when he publishes it: this is why the vast majority of children's dreams do not resemble the narratives published by renowned analysts.

THE ANALYST HELPS YOUNG CHILDREN
TO DISCOVER AND TELL THEIR DREAMS

Because he only conducted adult analyses, Freud used examples of dreams he had observed in his own children. It was with his youngest daughter that Freud managed to carry out a true reconstruction on behalf of the child. He used some words that she had uttered in her sleep to reconstitute her experience. When she was nineteen months old, she had had an attack of vomiting. She had been given nothing to eat for an entire day. During the night after this fasting, she had been heard shouting during her restless sleep: 'Anna Fweud, stwawbewwies, wild stwawbewwies, omblet, pudden!'[1] According to her father, his child had taken revenge in her sleep. The maid had attributed her illness to eating a large plateful of strawberries.

Freud long maintained that young children's dreams were short, clear, coherent, easily comprehensible and unambiguous. However, he conceded that distortions could occur in older children's dreams. Other analysts had reported to him dreams they had observed in their own children or their young patients. Freud then realised that children aged five to eight years old could have dreams that were as distorted as those of adults. In 1925, he recognised that at a fairly early age young children begin to have more complicated and less clear dreams than he had imagined possible.

What is striking about these very young children's dreams is the importance of the adult's contribution. Freud served as a true alter ego by helping the child to think, articulate in words and produce a narrative. The same procedure is found in one of the first child analyses reported by Melanie Klein. Since children have no means of using analysable material, adults have deployed aspects of waking life that they have in common with children.

Erich

Melanie Klein achieved a major advance when Erich, her youngest son, was nearly five years old. She considered the dreams and stories made up by her son and patient as the principal means of access to his unconscious phantasies. Guided entirely by her intuition, Klein sought to alleviate the child's anxiety through direct interpretations. She observed that Erich was extremely reluctant to revisit his fears by telling her what had been troubling him during the night. One day she managed, by putting some pressure on the child, to obtain the account of a dream that had frightened him very much. I shall consider this one because it resembles the narratives that we encounter nowadays in psychotherapy.[2] During the day, Erich had been looking at a picture-book that showed some men riding on horseback. In the night, he had seen the book open and two men come out of it. The child, and his brother and sister (both older than he) tried to cling to their mother. They gave up and ran away. They arrived at the front door of a house. A woman told them: 'You can't hide in here.' They hid in the house nonetheless and the men were unable to find them.

Klein chose to give an incomplete interpretation in order to avoid overstimulating the child. She used the only clue provided by Erich: the men were holding sticks, guns and bayonets. She explained to him that these objects represented Daddy's big willy that he both wished for and feared. Erich retorted to her: 'the weapons were hard but the wiwi is soft'.[3] Klein explained to the child that the willy would also become hard in connection with what he wanted to do with it. The child seemed to accept the interpretation. He added that it had seemed to him at times that one of the men had stuck into the other, so that there was then only one man.

Klein concluded that this was an early manifestation of homosexual impulses that had been little in evidence hitherto. She found confirmation of this in a subsequent dream. There were wolves everywhere with long tongues hanging out behind the mirrors, doors and so on. The dreamer shot at all the wolves with his gun and they died. He felt reassured at finding he was stronger than them. Erich was portraying his unconscious phantasies not only in his dreams at night but also in stories he invented during the daytime. Klein described these dreams as partly dreams and partly stories because Erich would sometimes begin by talking about a story that he had been told and sometimes with a nocturnal dream. She had noticed that the child's fears seemed to diminish while he was listening to the Grimms' fairy tales. Freud emphasised the important part that fairy tales can play in the child's psychic life. Elements and situations originating from these stories also sometimes appear in adults' dreams.

THE ANALYST MAGNIFIES HIS INTERPRETATION WHEN HE PUBLISHES IT

Analysts have often 'overinterpreted' young children's dreams when they have published them. Various interpretive layers have become superimposed over the course of time, just as an artisan applies lacquer to what will become a valuable object. The interpretation could be reworked because analyst and patient would meet five or six times a week in accordance with the practice at that time. Furthermore, interpretations can be revised outside the sessions. Many analysts still undertake an individual or group supervision. They run or attend seminars. Finally, a well-known analyst usually publishes a clinical case after having presented it in a lecture.

Richard

I shall now give an example of this type of over-interpretation that can occur among famous practitioners. This is a rather unusual paper published by Klein shortly before her death in 1960, in which she provides a detailed account of an analysis that had lasted only four and a half months. The mother had sought psychotherapeutic help for Richard when he was three years old. He was displaying disturbing behaviour following a circumcision. His mental balance had deteriorated further as he grew older. When he went to see Klein, his fear of other children was preventing him from attending school. The aerial bombardments in London had exacerbated his many fears.

The analysis took place in 1941. Then aged ten years old, Richard was suffering from a combination of persecution anxiety and depressive symptoms. Unlike most children of his own age, he preferred talking and thinking to playing. At the beginning of the ninth session, Richard put an important question to his analyst: could she help him to stop having dreams? He explained to her that he was always having terrible dreams.[4] Richard began to talk about some of his dreams. On one occasion, the queen from *Alice in Wonderland* was putting him to sleep with ether (the child had been put to sleep with ether before his circumcision). Another time, a German troop-carrier came right up to him. On another occasion, an old, black, abandoned car with lots of number-plates had moved towards him and stopped at his feet.

As he told his dreams, Richard had constantly been switching the electric fire off and on. In the previous session, he had already expressed the conflict associated with his jealousy of Klein's children and husband by operating this same switch. Klein began to interpret by connecting the dream with the session. The electric fire was black when it was switched off. It might then appear to be dead. The old, black car also looked dead. Richard pointed out to her that when the fire was on something red could be seen moving inside it.

Klein then modified her interpretation in terms of the combined parents phantasy. She told him that he wanted to stop the red thing that was moving inside the electric fire, the heat source representing the mother's body. However, if he attacked Daddy inside Mummy and destroyed him, Mummy might also die. He was afraid that if his attack were successful, he would find himself with an old, black, abandoned mother; that is, dead like the car in the dream.

The session continued. Klein was able to continue to interpret because of the associations. She showed him that he was feeling the same fear towards her, in the form of enemy troop-carriers (Richard knew that Klein came from Austria, a country allied with Germany and with which England was at war). When he had been put to sleep with ether for the operation, the mother had become malevolent by hiding the truth from him. He had felt that she was allied with the malevolent doctor. In *Alice in Wonderland*, the queen has people's heads cut off. She symbolises the bad mother and the bad father. In a dream, they had become the parents who wanted to cut off his genitals while he was asleep.

By confiding his fears, he had obtained some reassurance. Along with the cruel Austrian enemy, another part of Mrs Klein had been identified with the nurse, the only person who had wanted to protect him when he was facing many enemies (in his phantasies). Klein and her followers have been criticised for talking too much during a session and giving a constant stream of interpretation, as it were. Her account may lend some credence to these criticisms because it consists not in verbatim notes but in a reconstruction. Analysts have a tendency to emphasise their work and to remember only part of the material.

The vast majority of children's dreams cannot be interpreted as fully as this. In the example cited, the ten-year-old Richard was capable of talking about some nightmares that dated back to when he was three years old or at least of elaborating the memory of the traumatic experience caused by the circumcision. This is a highly intelligent, motivated and curious ten-year-old attending sessions six times a week. This first dream was told to an exceptional analyst who worked on the child's account over the course of several years.

THE ANALYST OFTEN HAS TO DRAW ON HIS OWN PSYCHIC RESERVES TO ENABLE THE INFANT TO COMMUNICATE THE DREAM NARRATIVE

The discrepancy between a published analysis and an ordinary session becomes clear if we compare the above example with those that follow. The comparison is particularly easy to make because this pre-adolescent child is retrieving the memory of an old nightmare.

Jacques

Jacques' mother brought him to see me when he was thirteen years old because he was having relational difficulties. 'As soon as he gets to school, he enters a minefield.' His only sister had been born fifteen months after him. According to his mother, he was fond of her. However, he would play tricks on her: for example, he had put drawing-pins on her head and shoved her on the stairs. At our first meeting, I helped him to recover the memory of a nightmare that must have occurred shortly after this intolerable birth. 'A witch had pushed me into a hole. Tarantulas (black or brown ones) were crawling all over me.' His inner world had changed so little since then that on the brink of adolescence he was afraid of holding the witch-puppet.

Claude

Another example with a young child presents us with a fairly ordinary reconstruction. Claude was six years old when her mother brought her to see me for a reason connected with school. However, a dramatic series of events had occurred in the family before and after her birth. It had not yet been possible to talk about these. When I asked Claude if she could tell me one of her dreams, she remembered an old nightmare. A witch was coming to torment her; she was wearing red clothes and a pointed hat. Claude hid under the table but the witch found her there. She could not recall how the dream ended. Claude agreed to play with the witch-puppet. She very quickly started a fight between the witch and the wolf. She had difficulty pretending and the wolf went flying into the middle of the room.

AFTER THE SECOND WORLD WAR, PSYCHOANALYTIC CASE STUDIES BEGAN TO INCORPORATE QUANTITATIVE RESEARCH

In 1937, Despert conducted a study in a nursery school in New York. Her objective was to assess the role played by dreams in personality development among apparently normal children. In the course of this research, nearly 200 dreams from around forty children aged between two and five years old were studied. Despert had been struck by the simplicity of the young children's dreams. In my view, not all children's dreams give this impression of simplicity. This generally characterises the dreams of children who are undergoing an effective process of mentalisation.

The emergence of language constitutes a fundamental stage in the construction of dream narratives. At around five years old, children become better able to articulate the narrative and to distinguish between dreams, imaginative play and reality. However, very young children are capable of portraying the content of their dreams through their bodily expressions and actions, even if they do not often manage to communicate this content verbally. However, it is still necessary to ascertain that the scenario has been represented during sleep.

It is difficult to picture the work carried out by the observer or therapist before any 'simplicity' in the narrative can be achieved. To demonstrate to the reader the close collaboration that occurs between adult and child, I shall discuss the account given by Despert.[5] I have chosen this interaction because I sometimes use the same procedure with young children or older children who are experiencing a block in their mental development. This child, of nursery-school age, spontaneously reported the following dream while he was playing with some dolls.

The boy started by saying:

'One time when I was sleeping, I saw ... (lowers his voice) ... a sly old fox.[6] It was real ...' ('A sly old fox?') 'A sly old fox, and a seal too.' ('And a seal?')

'*Yes ... (with an excited voice) ... yes, and when ... when ... when the seal come down, came down, he didn't bite me. When the fox came down, he bi ... he bi ... he didn't bite me. He said "I'm going to eat you up."*' ('*He did?*') '*I said "I'll ...," I said "I'll ... I'll shoot you with my gun."*' ('*When was that?*') '*It was a long time.*' ('*Was it in the night, or during the day? When was it?*') '*It was in the night, during the night.*' ('*During the night?*') '*Yeah.*' ('*Were you sleeping or were you awake?*') '*I was sleeping.*' ('*Was it a dream, or was it just thinking?*') '*... It was real.*' (*The child obviously means that it was real in the dream.*) ('*Oh, it was real – I see.*')[7]

The child then mentioned that there were boards in the ceiling. The observer concluded that these must be exposed beams. The child had been surprised on waking up not to find these in his bedroom when they had been so 'real' in his dream. *This demonstrates how widely the outcome of the dream experience can vary according to the person to whom the child is talking.* No one would have known this dream in detail if the child had not been with an interlocutor who had been made receptive by her analytic training and objective through a lack of personal involvement. Despert continued to talk with the child in her concern only to establish the parameters of the dream experience. If she had been acting as a psychotherapist instead of a researcher, she might instead have sought to establish a connection between the boards (with its theatrical reference) and the animals. She might have wondered if the seal and the fox had come down from the ceiling because they were angry at having been observed in their show on the boards.

In 1949, Despert produced a general survey of the publications in the English language (including English translation). Many of her findings remain valid to this day. At that time, child psychoanalysis had become widespread. Although it still held sway among professionals, it was no longer the sole source of inspiration. There had also been Piaget's work in particular, as we will see later on. Furthermore, the method used in individual cases was being counterbalanced by cohort studies of children. Despert had not merely produced a survey of the literature. She had also revealed the results of the 'quantitative research' that she had conducted as the leader of a team.

The main interest of the New York study resides in the analysis of the dream material that appears in young children's dreams. *Despert distinguished three categories among the figures that appeared: people, animals and inanimate objects.* People appeared more often than the other two types. Young children usually see their parents in dreams. They are generally either getting the child out of trouble or providing him with some form of (predominantly oral) gratification. Despert emphasised that the parents are not attacking or frightening the child. The opposite applies to other human beings, who appear to be wilfully destructive. The larger they are in size, and the more formidable their powers, the more destructive they are. There are sometimes supernatural creatures, including witches, ghosts and vampires.

The animals behave in a sadistic or even devastating way. They are characterised first by what they do to the child: they are biting (orality as always in early childhood) or chasing him while threatening his life. There is a very wide spectrum of animals, ranging from pets (dogs, cats, horses) to wild animals (lions, tigers, elephants) and including imaginary animals (wolves, werewolves and, more recently, dinosaurs).

Then there are the inanimate objects. These may only appear in the background but they can assume a living form and take part in the action by displaying human reactions. This transformation of inanimate objects in everyday life is particularly successful in many cartoons. Tex Avery has demonstrated this to adults with some genius.

Despert observed that young children rarely reported their dreams spontaneously. She referred to a 'segregation of emotional experiences'.[8] Not only do children tend to forget their dreams and what they have said about them; they also tend to be upset if they are reminded about them. Despert argued that the dream has a protective function. She attributed this protective forgetting solely to repression. This explains the general absence of direct references to sexuality. The dream also serves as a receptacle for discharging anxiety or aggression that would be intolerable in waking consciousness. Despert overlooked the splitting that plays a primordial role in early childhood. The earliest form of defence consists in splitting people into 'goodies' (the fairy) and 'baddies' (the witch). It is only gradually that splitting gives way to repression.

2
Playing, Maybe Dreaming

The child plays by using symbolic representations that enable him to gain some distance from his fears and his phantasies. Self-expression using toys and drawings is less conducive to anxiety than confiding something verbally. Klein had the inspired idea of analysing play in the same way as dreams. *Through play, children can simultaneously deploy both rational thought and a primitive thought that resembles the kind that occurs in dreams.* It is this dual encoding that often provides the key to interpreting play and understanding phantasies and conflicts.

I shall be giving an insight into what takes place between a psychotherapist and a child in therapy sessions. This type of work presupposes a level of psychic intimacy having been established, which deepens when the child plays, draws or tells his dreams. This process depends primarily on the way in which everything follows on and fits together in sequence. Klein discovered that children express through their play, activities and behaviour that which adults communicate in words. Children at play make fewer deliberate choices than adults do when they reflect.

CREATIVE PLAY CONFERS THE MEANING
OF THE DREAM ON THE WORLD

Winnicott modified play analysis by moving the emphasis from decoding the dream content to the experience of the dream. During play, the child sets about shaping a part of the external world. He confers on it the 'meaning and feeling' of the dream.[1] *The child during creative play is carrying out something equivalent to the dream work.* Many children who are referred for therapeutic consultations do not have a highly developed dream work or its equivalent: creative play. They first need to be helped to establish better internally the good enough mother's capacity for reverie.

Leo

Leo and his mother came to see me about his enuresis. He was just over seven years old. His father had peed in the bed until late in childhood, as had his mother. She had two children from a previous relationship. The elder child had also peed in the bed until a very late stage. Leo denied any jealousy towards his younger brother. However, he had been found to have an allergy in the year of this birth; he had also had many attacks of asthmatiform bronchitis and had undertaken some courses of hydrotherapy. Apart from this chronic enuresis, Leo gave every impression of being well and developing normally. At the end of our first meeting, I had helped him to talk about an indistinct memory relating to an old nightmare.

Three months later, I managed to see Leo with his father. We talked about his own father, whom he had not seen since his marriage. Encouraged by some talk about his father's late enuresis, Leo made a connection between his enuresis and his dreams. I then played with him alone. Not only did Leo not dare to take apart the toys; he was also unable to tolerate accidents that occurred. He constantly presented to all his interlocutors the very picture of goodness. He gave the impression of being completely incapable of naughtiness. With my guidance, he recognised that his mother would not have tolerated any displays of aggression on his part. His aggression surfaced only when it was disguised as passivity.

A few weeks later, Leo managed to give a detailed account of the nightmare that at our first meeting had only been mentioned. He thought he had had the nightmare when he was around three years old. A witch and a vampire were coming to take him away. I encouraged him to express himself by drawing a vampire's head with two blood-stained teeth. Then two wolves came along and bit its buttocks. Leo remembered that he had got up the night before. While still half-awake, he had been unable to find his bearings in the bedroom. He had released his faeces, believing himself to be in the loo.

The best can sometimes be the enemy of the good. Leo reminded me that he had an allergy because he had a cold that day. I thought that he meant he was afraid that this inner turmoil might precipitate a return of his asthma attacks. We then played with some plasticine. He wanted to make a building. I simply made a small man with a large willy. I gave Leo a pair of scissors. He hesitated before cutting the willy and then chopping it to pieces. Leo destroyed the little man to stop him from suffering. He then made a totem pole, an Indian one. My new little man found himself tethered to the torture post. Leo seemed to be inhabited by fairly shapeless and deeply repressed sadistic phantasies that nevertheless manifested themselves at night in a masochistic form.

Leo wanted to go on drawing. He loved drawing. He showed some talent here, particularly with war scenes. That day, Leo began by drawing a completely black American war-plane that was flying over the sea. The plane began to shoot in all directions. It gave me the impression of spitting, pissing and shitting but Leo was reluctant to talk about excrement. The plane attacked a Japanese patrol-boat. He explained what he was thinking by adding a bubble: 'Make the most of your last few minutes.' He then added a huge aeroplane that fired its ammunition relentlessly.

A few months later, Leo no longer hesitated to commit to paper fights taking place between himself and me. He still exhibited the same goodness and the familiar smile. That day, he began by drawing a gun-fight between two cowboys, one in blue and the other in black. He finally recognised with a laugh that he was the cowboy in blue and I was the one in black. He had insisted on explaining that this was only a game. He began by shooting a bullet through my stomach. I responded by just managing to graze his head. He ridiculed me by giving me pathetic characters as allies: one forgot to load his gun while another dropped his weapon when a sand-bag landed on his head.

Having completed this progressive drawing – a set of images that constituted an entire screen-play, Leo remembered a dream. 'I was driving a lorry. As I approached a petrol station, I turned the steering wheel.' I was then so surprised that I wondered if I might have misheard him. Leo had uttered the word 'suicide'. This made it difficult for him to talk about it. He evaded my questions. He said only that he knew exactly what it felt like to be about to die. I simply suggested a connection between the dream and the drawing: I thought questioning him might make him want to kill or lead him to destroy his head, as the source of his thoughts.

I remembered a session that had ended with our managing to talk with his father about his own mother's tragic death. She had burned to death in a fire in her house. Her mental capacities seemed to have deteriorated through illness. Leo was listening. He did not seem to know about this incident. This death had been followed by his parents' marriage and then his birth. There were yet more dreams and many drawings with different heroes. Leo left me after two and a half years of therapy sessions. He was still peeing in bed but intermittently. He was expressing his aggression more effectively. I had helped him to deal with a major conflict with one of his female teachers.

Klein seems to have been interested primarily in psychic reality and the relationship that develops between psychic and external reality. Winnicott

emphasised an 'intermediate realm' of experience in which both inner reality and external life play a part. This experience corresponds to the transition experienced by young children when they move from a primary state of union with their mother to a relationship with her in which they are a separate entity. Transitional phenomena provide all human beings from the outset with a psychic place that enables them both to connect and to separate external reality and shared reality.

I was able to help Leo because he and his parents were willing to reconstitute the illusion that had existed in very early childhood, which is also an intrinsic part of cultural production. There are dangers attached to the failure to recognise and accept external reality. In adults, expecting to exercise too much power over others and forcing them to participate in an excessively emotional illusion is a sign of madness. Winnicott considered transitional phenomena to be normal and universal. However, he conceded that some pathologies – drug addiction, fetishistic perversion, lying and theft – might resemble a corruption of these phenomena.

LIKE DRAWING, PLAY REPRESENTS
WHAT IS HAPPENING IN THE INNER WORLD

The therapist seems to oscillate between two attitudes to children's drawings. The classical view leads him to articulate the unconscious phantasy when it emerges in the representation. Another more recent approach addresses both the form and the content of the representation, as with dreams. It considers the mentalisation of transference phantasies. Like drawing, play relates to the dream work, but to a dream based on material originating from the mental functioning within the patient–therapist pair.

Jerome

Jerome was brought to see me when he was six and a half years old for encopresis. He was so constipated that he would release pieces of hard faeces when he played sport. Jerome had almost become clean when the birth of a brother, who was two years younger than him, had thrown everything into doubt. Some consultations with a psychologist when he was three years old had done nothing to remove the symptoms. His mother was making a further attempt because another brother, who was five years younger, had been born the year before. Jerome was doing well at school. He already knew how to read by the time he started at school. However, he was throwing fits at home when he was too tense. He was also hitting his younger brother.

Jerome had had nightmares when he was eighteen months old. During this period, his mother was pregnant with his younger brother. He was seeing demons. As a result, his mother had stated: 'He can read my mind; he also reads his younger brother's mind.' Jerome did in fact sometimes finish his mother's or his brother's sentences for them. His mother had traced this back to the paternal great-grandmother who had been telepathic. Jerome had the same cowlick as her on his forehead at the root of his hair. Jerome had modestly concurred with this. He had given a similar response when she stated that he was producing some very beautiful drawings.

This mother had provided so much information that she had taken up almost the entire session (there had been a particular question about a conflict concerning a court ruling that had designated the father as his own father's guardian). In the course of this conversation, Jerome had produced a beautiful drawing based on his favourite game, which involved soldiers on horseback and a fortified castle. Jerome explained this clearly: he and his brother were at war. Large numbers of soldiers were coming down the mountains to join the knight with his banner. It was an invading army. The mother had told me that Jerome believed his ancestors had been knights.

We talked about nightmares at the very end. Jerome would have these if he did not have two cuddly toys with him: a bear and a leopard. 'When I don't have them, I see demons. (Why are you frightened?) They frighten me when they quarrel.' When we parted, I had promised him to devote myself especially to him the next time. In the following session, Jerome came with his father, who had insisted on meeting me. He accepted that the child was expressing something through his symptoms. He recognised that he and his wife had not been well during the pregnancy and at the time of the birth. Jerome's grandfather had been seriously ill. The father returned late in the evenings because of his work. He had been feeling better since going to see a psychiatrist himself.

Jerome was pleased to see me again. He had started drawing while I was talking with his father. This time, he had chosen the sea, a Viking ship with a warrior at the front. A whale was leaping. It was going to be caught. I do not know what happened next because Jerome stopped drawing as soon as his father left. In answer to my question, he told me a recent dream.

I had the impression that he was talking about a daydream that was based on a nocturnal dream. 'There were some knights like in the films. They are attacking. (And you?) I am the king. (What are you doing?) I am attacking a king because he wanted my castle. There is a great wall that is called Dragon. Because if you look at it from above, it is the shape of a dragon.' I tried to make a connection with his brother, as in the previous session, but to no avail.

'Sometimes, he makes me cry. This morning, he pushed the table while I was drawing.'

The next time, Jerome drew a knight who was mounting a horse covered in a purple caparison before engaging in combat with his lance. He told me that he always had the same dream. I asked him to tell it to me all the same. I heard a different version. 'It starts with a war. There is a child who is hiding. He is going to grow up and that will be me. The war lasts ten years. One day, I arrive in order to fight. I kill the bad men with my army. Then I have some children. At the end, I die.'

Events then took a different turn because I introduced a *deus ex machina*. A paediatric consultation led to a period in hospital. Jerome has nearly completely stopped defaecating in his pants. Fortunately, the paediatrician knew me, and he insisted that they should not abandon the therapy when the embarrassing symptom disappeared. I continued to see Jerome and his parents. The family situation had also improved. The father had managed to re-establish contact with his own father. The children were able to see their grandfather in their own house. Finally, the family moved into a bigger house.

I recorded the dream that Jerome had had before the move. 'There is a knight. He is made of stone. Before, it was a large rock. The stone was transformed. A little man came out of it. As soon as he put on his armour, he became a man. He had golden lions on his armour and a feather in his helmet. As soon as he drew on the ground with his sword, it became a real lion. He was not bad; nor were the men. (And you, were you in the dream?) I was the knight.' Looking back on this, I felt worried. Jerome must have been experiencing some prolonged difficulties during which he might have fallen into a deep depression or felt depersonalised. Contrary to his usual practice, Jerome did not draw. He had brought his toys. He also used the toys in the session. But the lion in the game was not kind like the one in the dream. It attacked a horse and ate it. The knights split into two groups that attacked and savagely killed each other.

One year later, we decided to discontinue the therapy. At the last session, Jerome spent almost all his time drawing while taking inspiration from a recurrent dream. 'I saw in my dream that this dragon was a great wall.' Jerome produced a highly complex drawing with some views from an aeroplane and representations that were unusual for his age. Jerome began with the dragon-wall. He then drew on this outline the map of a city with housing blocks, houses, a (yellow) temple and its (orange) palace. 'A dragon was attacking a great wall. All the animals rushed at the wall. The dragon was kind at the end.' I asked him who was there. 'I am a prince. I have a father who is living in a shark-wall.' Jerome covered the page with combatants of every kind. He planned the movements in his head before committing them to paper.

UNDERSTANDING A DREAM OR A DRAWING IS BASED ON EMOTIONAL SHARING BETWEEN THE CHILD AND THE ADULT

A child's case is easier to publish if it is accompanied by beautiful or moving drawings. The drawing constitutes the only material trace that can be communicated to an audience or to readers. However, drawing is also interesting in itself. It brings into play the psychic capacity for symbolisation during waking life. It enables what is happening in the inner world to be presented in a visual form.

Émilien

Émilien had just had his tenth birthday; he was about to start at secondary school. His mother had 'dragged' him to see me because he was suffering from insomnia. I noticed that I was one of a long list of professionals destined to remain rather helpless. He had always had difficulties with sleeping. 'He is over-anxious', his mother had explained. The beginning of the current episode dated back to the changing of the clocks several months earlier. The mother had informed me that she and her husband were 'great sleepers'. Émilien was afraid at night. He would listen out for noises. He did not hesitate to go into his parents' bedroom at any time.

Although he had shown some reluctance to come, Émilien talked easily with me. As his mother almost completely forbade him to watch television, he read. He told me about something he had been reading about a child who received a shrunken head as a present from one of his aunts. The child went to the island from which the head had originated. He discovered that he had had supernatural powers since he had undergone hypnosis. Émilien started to draw a head with a pencil. He had surprised me by beginning with the bridge of the nose and the eyebrows. He acknowledged that he was having nightmares. However, he did not want to talk about them. He finally related to me the one he had previously told to a psychologist, whom his mother had taken him to see when he was three years old because of some 'fits'. I was not able to discover anything more about their nature. However, I had noted that this was the period during which his mother had been pregnant with Émilien's sister.

'I am in a friend's bedroom. (He does not know which friend. He is partly in the picture but the main focus is on the friend.) I ask him: "Have you ever been burgled?" He replies: "no". I was about to say: "nor have I". Just then, a dagger came through the door that was ajar (he got up to act the scene).' Émilien then made a surprising connection with a dream that he had had the night before. 'I

seem to remember that I was with Manon (she is exactly the same age as me, she is my father's brother's daughter).' Then Émilien drew a dagger above the head. When his mother came back, he drew a skull at the bottom of the drawing. I discovered that he used to draw a lot of skeletons and skulls.

Winnicott devised the *squiggle* game mainly as an aid for latency-age children. Its importance resides not in the opportunity it provides to doodle and scribble in the presence of an adult but in the way in which the therapist becomes involved on the same level as the child. They work together to produce a drawing that subsequently reveals a problem or an emotional conflict that is surfacing at that moment. Understanding dreams, like drawing with someone, brings about some emotional sharing between the child and the therapist. Producing a drawing with someone or telling a dream requires trusting them and agreeing to share some psychic intimacy.

Joint drawing seems to me to open the way to dreams. It provides the primary experience in which creativity emerges with a new opportunity for transformation. It is through play that the child can be creative and discover his deep

1

personality. This creativity will be integrated into his personality if it is reflected as in a mirror, which is only possible if someone who is empathetically disposed sends back an image of it. Joint drawing is an activity that is equally far removed from the representation of the internal mother, who is almost under magical control, and the real mother, who eludes almost every form of control.

I am going to mention only one series of joint drawings. In (1) Émilien began by drawing what looked to me like a snake. He drew the mouth of a man who was about to eat something. This became a rather horrible creature with a scar, a bandage and an earring. In (2) I drew a wavy line that he made into a kite. I added some lightning striking it. He took the electric current down to the bottom of the picture, where he put some sticks of dynamite. In (3) he drew a violet oval shape that I made into a flying saucer. He accepted my idea. At the bottom, he drew a terrified man running away. He drew an extra-terrestrial creature coming down from the flying saucer. In (4) I drew two connected oval shapes. He made them into a face. I added a ghost as a form of nose. He described the whole thing as a teacher looking closely at a ghost. (I also asked him if that was me because I wear glasses.)

One day, Émilien's mother attempted to reflect while talking with me in front of her son. She had noticed that her son's insomnia had returned while she had been in hospital for a surgical operation. It was the first time that she had had an operation and that they had been apart. He had also left to go to ski school the following month. His father was going for some treatment the next day to have some prosthetic material removed from his fractured leg. Émilien slept badly when his mother was out in the evenings. He went to join his father in his bed. She had concluded from this that the 'umbilical cord' had not yet been cut. She then took him (without consulting me) to see a sleep specialist and then a microkinesis practitioner. Émilien was finally able to sleep at night or to get up without disturbing his parents.

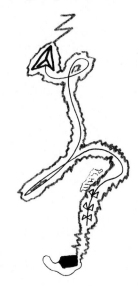

2

3

One day, Émilien's mother told me that he was having difficulty sleeping again. He had fractured his arm in several places and had had to have an operation. I found it understandable that he should have had some difficulty getting to sleep but she did not. Émilien was a charming boy who seemed well in himself; he was intelligent, doing well in his studies and had a gift for drawing. He told me a final dream before we parted. 'My maternal grandmother was there. (She lives near them. He sees her several times a week. Her husband died long before the grandson was born.) She found some innards and a brain in her cellar. She shouted: "Come and look at this!" I thought she had seen a dead rat. We (my mother and I) went to look. We saw it; we were revolted. I awoke with a start.' Émilien did not give me any associations and the dream has lost none of its mystery.

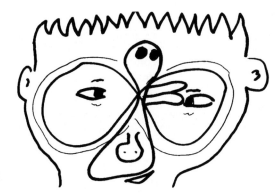

4

3
Adolescents and Dreams

Adolescence is an important stage of human development because it forms the transition from childhood to adulthood. In reviewing it, we tend to focus sometimes on the child and sometimes on the adult rather than the adolescent. Adolescents find themselves battling simultaneously on two fronts: externally, they have to separate and differentiate themselves from their parents while also adopting some of their characteristics. However, internally, they still feel a nostalgia for the images of childhood. They cannot acquire an adult identity without becoming part of a genealogy, but they cannot grow up without challenging and destroying.

In general, adolescence involves the experience of crises. This atmosphere of crisis has been explained using two analogies: on the one hand, with psychotic states and, on the other, with borderline states. Some regard psychotic manifestations as a general characteristic that is observable in adolescence, citing three aspects of the reorganisation that occurs at that time: the role of the body, the search for identity, and the balance between cathexis of the self and cathexis of others. These are aspects of every psychotic process. The similarity with borderline states (between psychosis and neurosis) is even more self-evident. Some even maintain that the adult borderline state is fundamentally no different from the adolescent state.

Dreams are no exception to this general pattern of changes: there is a gradual transition from childhood dreams to adult dreams. *This raises an interesting question as to the 'function of dreams'.* It is a premise of classical psychoanalytic theory that the dreamer has the capacity to repress, symbolise and carry out the dream work. However, this does not apply to psychotic and borderline personalities nor to psychotic components present in neurotics. Following Bion, it has been observed that a patient can use a dream to evacuate rather than to elaborate parts of his self and his internal objects.

Ladame has argued that dreams and actions are inseparable in adolescence and that they constitute its principal safety-valve.[1] The adolescent psyche is riven with conflicting impulses. On the one hand, the signs of sexual potency have to be integrated while the temptation to incest and murder is avoided; on the other hand, there is a need to accept that the unconscious desires of childhood will always endure in the psyche. The psychic transformations that are triggered by puberty have to modify the reality principle by carrying out unbinding processes that enable new bonds to be established.

The dream is a model for the psychic activity of binding. Setbacks or failures in the dream work can bring an exposure to drive pressures that may assume a traumatic dimension. This protective function in the psychic apparatus also applies to action (in that it hinders a simple motor discharge).

HOW THE PSYCHIC SPACE OF THE DREAM
EXPANDS AT ADOLESCENCE

High-risk situations can arise when there is a delay in the formation of new associations following dangerous unbindings. The following account provides an example of this.

Anne

Anne, who was twelve and a half years old, had been referred to me by a paediatrician for bulimic tendencies and frequent crying, along with a mother who was blaming herself.[2] It soon became clear to me that all this was related to the mother's fourth pregnancy. The therapeutic consultation provided the opportunity to address the conflict about parenthood with the elder daughter while taking a preventive measure with regard to the future baby. The mother was able to undertake a course of psychotherapy herself after the birth.

The therapy sessions continued for nearly two years. The birth of another daughter had painfully revived Anne's conviction that she had not been sufficiently loved. Resorting to the same solution as in the past, she regressed. However, because of pubertal urges she thought about replacing her mother rather than taking the baby's place. I was able to help Anne to come to terms with the past and confront her conflicts associated with psychic bisexuality. She provided many dreams and joint drawings in our meetings.

I am going to present just a few extracts that I find particularly significant. At our first meeting, I had concluded that life must have been difficult for her as a baby because of her parents' relative youth, as they were still students, from different countries, who had just moved house. Her mother had told me about Anne's first day at nursery school: 'The separation was difficult both for her and for me. But she liked the school.' Anne immediately qualified this by telling me: 'When school is over, I have a nightmare. The school is burning down but I always escape.'

Most of her dreams involved either sequences of events connected with school or scenes from family life. One day, Anne told me that her parents were tired of having their youngest daughter in their bedroom. They were planning to build on. However, meanwhile, they had to make some changes because the flat was too small for each child to have her own room. Anne asked my advice: should she agree to share her bedroom with Virginie, her sister who was eighteen months younger? Anne seemed to be willing to accept her former rival, towards whom she was feeling less hostile.

Anne then told me a recent dream: 'A car was running over Virginie's cat.' This dream was not entirely displeasing to Anne because this cat had peed in her bedroom. Also, it reserved its 'turbo-charge' purring for Virginie. Anne heard that this cat was on heat. She was surprised because she thought that only female cats had this condition. I asked Anne if she might have been driving the car that ran over the cat: 'No, no!' Besides, she did not remember her dreams. She did not remember her mother's dreams either, which her mother recorded for her psychotherapist. She would leave them lying around in places where anyone could read them.

We will move straight on to her last dream. Anne had just celebrated her fourteenth birthday. She told me that she would not be coming to see me any more. She would definitely not be there the following week. She was going to Italy with her school. She then told me her dream: 'I was leaving for Italy that night without having packed my suitcases and without my passport. At the border, they made us all go back to look for them.' Anne told me that she had in fact lost her passport and authorisation to leave the country. I asked her if this related to her identity as a child or an adolescent. I mentioned *Alice in Wonderland*, with which we were both familiar. Anne did not take in my question. She remembered (or invented) the end of the dream: 'I saw Mum packing my bags and I left again.'

Jeammet considers that the adolescent problematic resides mainly in the connection between internal reality and external reality.[3] He has proposed the term 'enlarged psychic space' for the arena in which this problematic is played out. Unsettled by the upheaval in his inner world, the adolescent needs those close to him to be willing to compensate for this or that psychic function. He strongly projects aspects of his inner world. The adult has a difficult role to play when confronted with these strong unconscious demands. He risks either refusing to be the object of the projection and repeating a traumatic moment or taking an attitude that reinforces the conviction that this is only about external reality.

HOW CHILDHOOD DIFFICULTIES CAN RESURFACE IN ADOLESCENT DREAMS

We have seen with Anne that her mother had embarked on a new pregnancy just as her daughter was beginning to be troubled by pubertal urges. This had fostered a massive and violent resurgence of the conflict-ridden situations of early childhood. I had had to demonstrate some caution in relation to the transference; I had used it rather than interpreted it. Anne perceived the parental couple as combined parents; that is, a mother who contains the father's penis in order constantly to engender new children. The dreams had provided some information concerning the state of object relations in this pre-adolescent girl. We are now going to consider another situation in which therapy sessions during adolescence made it possible to return to dreams experienced in childhood.

Paul

Paul was ten and a half years old when his mother brought him to see me about his tic. This had disappeared at the time we met. We only referred to it. It mainly affected his mouth and tongue. His mother felt that Paul was fearful and unsure of himself. He allowed his twin, who was in the same class, to dominate him.

Paul had replied that he fairly often had dreams. In one of them, a crocodile came to attack him while he was tied up.

Paul had produced a fairly clumsy drawing of a train and, in front of the locomotive, a stone wall. He had not been able to construct a story on the basis of his drawing. Paul seemed to have obsessional symptoms, in the form of anxious brooding and questioning. I suggested that he might do some relaxation exercises with a psychomotrician. He did this for a while. I saw his mother once more on her own, at the psychomotrician's request, because there were some major difficulties in her father's family. However, she had failed to understand my suggestion that she might have a consultation herself. She could communicate only about her son's suffering. Paul had had eczema and he was still asthmatic.

I was surprised when Paul came to see me again five years later. He had insisted on seeing me alone. He had become a tall, thin adolescent, who discomfited me with his questions. A month earlier, he had decided to watch a video alone, *The Silence of the Lambs*. He had been so disturbed by this that he had had trouble sleeping. He had not known that such a thing was possible. What? We tried to formulate the question together: that it was possible to take such pleasure in doing harm and to go so far beyond what was permitted; above all, however, that he might become like that himself one day.

Paul questioned me directly. He wanted me to tell him ... I could not predict what he would become. I encouraged him to talk about the present, adolescence and the changes that had taken place in his body. I reminded him about the past. His asthma attacks had stopped. His tic had disappeared. He had taken up karate. One day, he might become a policeman (like the heroine in the film?). He said he was average in his class. Like his twin, he had chosen foreign languages and they had been put in the same form for the fourth year. But the domination had stopped. Each twin led his own life and had his own friends.

When I asked him about this, Paul told me he was not having any dreams. He finally remembered a dream he had had when he was ten years old (around the time of his first consultation). 'It was as if I were a ghost. I had a sheet over me and I could only see white (because there were no eye-holes). A dog wanted to bite me (or did bite me). When I tried to move forward I was in a void.' I tried to make a connection between his current fears and his anxious brooding in the past. But he wanted to forget what he used to be like.

Paul had still insisted on being alone in the next session. He had seen the film *Seven* on television. He had felt disturbed but not in the same way. He remembered a dream he had had two weeks after seeing the film. 'I think that this might interest you ... It was a person with nothing but two legs and a sphere at the top – a sphere filled with electronic devices that enabled the legs to move forward. I think it was a woman who had had a car accident. She was in an auditorium in which some scientists and an audience were observing her. (And you?) I was also in the hall (my eye was guiding the "camera"). There were buttons with lights that showed it was working.'

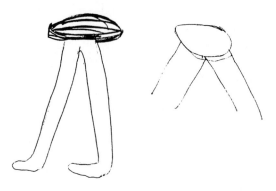

Not having seen the film, I felt disconcerted. I asked him if he could draw his dream. He drew two legs with a convex disc or a gaping mouth. I asked him if the woman still had the use of her excretory and sexual functions. And her pants? Yes, the sphere is a pair of pants full of electronic devices. I tried to relate his dream to his personal experience. Were these 'twin' legs? Perhaps he had imagined one day that his mother or his sister might have a car accident. 'When I was little, in bed, and my mother was coming home late, I used to imagine that she might have had an accident. Recently, my father did not turn up to collect me. My sister and I waited for an hour. When I walked back, I thought that he might have had a car accident.'

Paul then described to me a scenario in a film he had invented. 'Once, I imagined a horror film, the worst of all for me. There was a man like me. He was filled with straw, with a pointed hat, with sleeves that hid his hands … He was walking in a kind of desert (inhabited by Native Americans). He was moving forward slowly, rhythmically. (Why was that frightening?) What was horrible was that he could not see anything, could not feel anything, although he had a human form. The camera revealed his face, his body (a gesture to indicate zooming out) and then a tribe of Native Americans around him.'

Paul then remembered a dream he had had when he was five or six years old. 'It kept coming back. I was afraid … a spider-woman, this tall (a hand gesture indicating a height of forty centimetres above the desk), with brown hair, wearing black. It was a woman transformed into a black spider with a web around her. She was under my small desk. My bed was next to my desk. When I was lying in bed, I could see the desk and the spider under it. When I got up, she threw her web at me. She grabbed me and there was nothing I could do.' I suggested to him that the film had acted like a spider's web: he had been helplessly dragged into it. He agreed with this.

The next time, Paul told me that he was feeling better before starting to talk at top speed. 'It is almost as if I were a killer. I get this feeling in my throat or my stomach as if I were about to do it … It happens with people I love, a member of my family, but not friends … I think the film may have nothing to do with it. It happens when I'm not thinking about anything … When I was little, I used to hit my sister very hard. I put her under the bed-clothes. I trapped her, I wanted to suffocate her.' I tried to go back to his adolescence, his past, his situation with his twin. He refused to consider any of this.

I tried to make a connection between the urge to suffocate and the fear of suffocating. He replied that he had never been afraid of dying during his asthma attacks. However, he admitted: 'Perhaps it would be a relief to do that to someone.' He told me that he had made extraordinary progress in two years of karate. He sometimes found when he was fighting that he could not stop hitting. 'It is rather like an exorcism. I thought about committing suicide in order to stop doing it.' I suggested to him that there might be two parts struggling inside him and that one might take over the other. But he had lost interest in dreams. He said he was no longer having any. He did not want to come back again.

THE DREAM WORK CAN HELP TO OVERCOME INCESTUOUS IMPULSES AND THE ATTRACTION OF DEATH

In adolescence, the psyche gradually changes in structure over time. As they grow up, young people oscillate between contradictory attitudes. Just as the development of sexual characteristics could entail a serious risk of incest, the fascination with death involves some high-risk behaviour. If they have developed in an elaborative direction, dreams can help with overcoming the incestuous temptation and the attraction of death. The following example provides us with an insight into this.

Céline

Céline had just had her fourteenth birthday when her mother brought her to see me. She was deeply affected by the death of a friend. Eight months earlier, he had died in circumstances that seemed to indicate suicidal tendencies. When I was alone with Céline, I asked her if she knew any reasons for this delayed reaction. A distinct and rather cultish aura had developed around the vanished friend. His photograph, his scent, his judo belt and so on had become objects of veneration. This group reaction had initially prevented Céline from feeling the full force of the loss. However, she was becoming increasingly occupied with thoughts of going to join him. Céline often had dreams. She told me: 'I can see a white shape. I can make out the features of his face under the cloth … the shape is reaching out its hand to me. It wants to take me away.'

We did not talk only about the tragic event. We also discussed her personal problems. Céline was in the third year of secondary school after having repeated her second year. This failure at school had caused some upset in the family, which had led to family therapy being considered for a while. Céline was the eldest of four siblings and the only girl. She had generally sought out her father's company but recently she had become closer to her mother. Céline had also had eczema and was suffering from allergies and asthma.

This is the second and final dream that she told me: 'We had found a new planet in the solar system. Everyone who died on Earth came to live there... It was completely dark with craters. There was some mist... I finally found Marc. We went back to Earth in a rocket. Everything was just as it was before.' Céline was happy to have found her friend again in her dream but she now knew that he would never come back. She expressed some aggression towards the deceased, then a sense of guilt. Céline got through the fateful date of the first anniversary without difficulties and then she no longer needed to come to see me.

ADULTS SOMETIMES RESOLVE CHILDHOOD AND ADOLESCENT ISSUES THROUGH THEIR DREAMS

Specialists are divided about the problems experienced by adolescents. It is not known whether an adolescent can be treated in a single stage or if two stages have to be anticipated, the first in adolescence and the second in adulthood. The fact remains that hospital units have chosen to accept adolescents and young adults. Some reach adulthood while internally preserving a problematic that is partly related to difficulties in childhood and then in adolescence. It is important to find a way of giving them the opportunity of developing instead of withdrawing into themselves. The following example will provide some insight into this.

Carole

Although she was twenty and a half years old, Carole had chosen to consult a doctor who specialised in treating children. She thought that her present difficulties were connected with her childhood. She was studying in preparation for a career in sales and marketing. This had led on to a professional training course; it had gone badly. She had started being horrible to her boyfriend, who was slightly older than she was. There had also been much discussion about her parents. She had complained about her father's alternating presence and absence. She was angry with him about a long-standing extra-marital relationship.

I asked her if she was having any dreams. She finally remembered a dream that she had had five or six months previously. 'I was being judged by five dogs (two or three were dead, they were completely surrounding me). They were wearing wigs like English judges. (These were large dogs, like beaucerons). When I woke up, I felt I had been condemned, mainly because of the way in which the middle one was looking at me.' She had nothing to add to this. I pressed her and she told me: 'I was nearly bitten by my cousin's dog (the cousin was the daughter of my mother's sister, who died at the age of forty). I was on a swing. I must have been about ten years old. It was an Alsatian.'

We continued to talk as if Carole had forgotten her dream. This was only on the surface because she told me: 'The lecturer told me that I wanted to be as my father wanted, that I was too hard on myself. My boyfriend told me that I focused on other people's bad points ... Yes, he is more important than my father. He has been sleeping with me at home for four months. He sometimes helps me to make the first move.' I tried to make a connection. Carole might have been afraid of going to see clients because she would feel that she was behaving like her father's mistress. One day, she had turned up at their house unannounced. I wondered if she would come again and how she was going to react.

The next time, Carole was there. She preferred it if I asked her questions (like a judge?). Without giving it too much thought, I read her the account of her dream, which seemed to be crucial for her. This triggered some strong emotion. Carole then told me the dream that she had had on Saturday night. 'My mother was telling me that my brother was dead. Afterwards I felt ill. That is what woke me up.' Had anything happened that might have produced the thought in this dream? 'My boyfriend had to attend the anniversary of the death of a friend. He died in a car accident.' Carole had hardly mentioned her only brother until then, who was seventeen months younger. He was studying in a town in the region. He lived there in the week but came back home at weekends. He had a girlfriend.

Carole unconsciously gave me a sequel to the dream by telling me about an incident that had infuriated her that morning. She and her brother had to share a car that they had been given and that was maintained by their father. Their mother had announced: 'You are both forbidden to drive during the holidays.' Carole added: 'My mother had filled the petrol tank. My brother had had the car since the beginning of the holidays. He left it empty. I wanted to use the car and I couldn't. My brother thinks of no one but himself.'

I remembered the dream and asked her if she might wish for her brother's death. 'Yeah, sometimes I've felt that way. My mother always takes his side.' Carole knew that this went back a long way. 'My parents told me that when my mother came back from maternity hospital, I picked up a plastic bottle and hit her ... I started walking at the same time.' I asked her: 'You can go faster in a car?' She smiled in agreement.

Our conversations continued. One day, Carole even drew a picture with me. She said she could not draw well. However, she gradually portrayed Lucky Luke, a half-male and half-female figure. There is too much material to relate here and a fragment of the discussion will be enough in conclusion. Carole began to look for some work for the summer. She wanted to improve her chances of being recruited by arranging some introductions for herself. She was disappointed, hurt by a woman telling her through a secretary that her husband did not have time to see her. We had rediscovered the disappointment in waiting in relation to a couple and the sense of not being valued.

The workings of memory had revived for her an event in the distant past. A few years ago, she had started going out in the evening. She would put on some make-up. Her father had told her that she was looking like a tart. She had found that idea of going out to sell her body intolerable. I asked her if her father might have been jealous because this was when she had started going out with her boyfriend. She was moved by my comment. She did not know why her father was so important to her. On the basis of several weeks of conversation,

I had suggested to her that after the birth of her brother she had been deeply disappointed in her mother and had turned to her father. Carole had again been very moved by this suggestion. I likened the father's condemnation to the condemnation by the central judge in the dream. What did she feel guilty of? She did not reply. She wondered if she could change. Other people would appreciate her more if she could love herself more. When we parted, Carole had grown up psychically. She no longer needed a children's doctor.

4
Ways of Dreaming in Childhood

Khan (a follower of Winnicott) has defined what he terms a 'good dream'.[1] This is a dream that incorporates an unconscious wish. It allows sleep to continue while remaining accessible to the ego's psychic experience once the dreamer has awoken. The more satisfactory care and support children have received from their environment, the better 'the experience of the dream' fosters their personality development.

Houzel has also put forward an interesting hypothesis concerning the connections between dreaming and psychopathology in children.[2] There is a broad variety of drive functioning: at the optimal end of the spectrum, it enables the self to connect with external objects in order to produce a mental representation of them that fosters psychic coherence. At the other end of the spectrum, drive functioning has a disorganising impact and weakens the internal coherence of the psyche by destroying the connections between external and internal objects. Similarly, dream activity can either contribute towards personality integration and resolution of inner conflicts or, alternatively, turn into an unbinding activity.

When a neurotic child manages to remember a dream, he makes associative connections. The latent content produces conflicts in its formulation as a narrative. The greater the child's personality disturbance, the more sharply these conflicts manifest themselves. When children with highly disorganised structures manage to produce a dream narrative, they are thereby demonstrating a significant improvement in their mental functioning.

AT FIRST, THE CHILD'S DREAMING
NEEDS TO BE INCUBATED BY THE MATERNAL REVERIE

The repression that operates in classical neuroses already presupposes a high level of mentalisation. Only material that has already been mentalised through an intersubjective matrix is subject to repression. Newborn children first have to transform the raw data of experience. They have to produce mental representations; that is, to develop and utilise stable mental images of a thing or a person instead of the thing or person themselves. This enables them to connect fundamental experiences with both images and words. They also have to symbolise; that is, to move from concrete to abstract thought.

In this book, I shall provide a review of dream theory that owes a great deal to Bion (who was Klein's most creative student). Bion considered 'maternal reverie' to be a component of both motherhood and psychotherapy. The mother is capable of a good enough reverie if she preserves and in some sense digests her child's intolerable emotions and experiences so that he can reintegrate them internally. These acquire a meaning when they are symbolised. To be communicated and imparted through speech, they must be linked in the form of a narrative.

Sensory impressions and emotions do not simply enter the human brain. They also have to undergo a fundamental transformation before they can acquire a psychic dimension and become a content of thought. In this sense, an experience that takes place during sleep is no different from an experience that occurs in the waking state. In both cases, the data of this experience have to be transformed before they can be used as dream thoughts.[3]

The mother's reverie develops on two complementary levels: emotional and intellectual. Through her empathy, she can recognise or guess the kind of emotions and feelings that her baby is experiencing. She assesses whether these need to be attenuated or counterbalanced. By responding to them appropriately, she helps the baby to discover what they are and, later, to find a name for them. The mother somehow pinpoints his most pressing need amid a jumble of helplessness and distress. The newborn baby gradually comes to internalise this way of proceeding and thinking by himself.

Pregnancy enables the mother to develop a primary maternal concern. She develops an intuitive capacity to sense the baby's needs. She can offer at the desired moment what he needs to live and develop. The maternal reverie is a specific form of daydream. Daydreams have some characteristics in common with nocturnal dreams. Typically, however, daydreams contain more coherent scenarios than nocturnal dreams.

However, reverie can also be a means of escaping or denying reality through fantasies. Winnicott observed that abnormal fantasmatic activity could occur in adults. The psychic apparatus then seeks only to expend energy, whereas in dreams it uses the imagination to enrich life. It goes without saying that the maternal reverie also has an enriching effect on the baby's mental life by filtering and regulating his emotions and providing him with meaning.

THE GREATER THE PREDOMINANCE OF PSYCHOSIS IN THE PERSONALITY, THE MORE NIGHTMARES CONTRIBUTE TO INTERNAL DISORGANISATION

The protagonist of Buten's first novel is a deeply disturbed child. The reader is able to feel some empathy with the child because the author has lent him his own capacity for understanding. However, this understanding does not extend to the nightmares: although these appear at the beginning and the end of the book, it is only possible to guess at their impact. The first discovery is a shocking one: the child killed himself when he was five years old by pointing his index finger at his temple and pushing it down with his thumb. His interior monologue soon brings the past back. Burton describes his daily life: 'I am scared of going to bed because there are monsters in my closet. I keep the door closed. The more times you push it the more closed it is. Before bed I push my closet door fifty times.'[4]

The book concludes with a letter that the child writes to Jessica, the little girl with whom he is in love. In it, he only makes passing reference to a dream. Burton cannot remember or talk about it. The reader may infer that the content must have been very frightening and that it related to the parental couple sleeping in their bedroom. We should remember that Burton had 'killed' himself at the age when he had the mysterious dream. 'Once I was five. It was summer. I got to stay up late because there wasn't school. And one night I had a bad dream. I woke up. It was all dark in my room. There was a shadow over the closet. Everything was quiet. I didn't feel good. I was sweating. It was cold on me. I sat up and waited. I waited and waited. Then I got out of bed. I pointed at the door and went. I walked into the hall in my pajamas. I stood in the hall next to the night-light in front of my parents' room. I listened. But I didn't hear anything. Inside of their room was black.'[5]

Psychoanalysis has shown that there are at least two ways of bringing the past back into the present: remembering and acting out. In the concept of acting out, Freud combined in an ambiguous way the satisfaction of drives, phantasies and desires and the recourse to motor action. When an adult embarks on an analysis, he agrees to enter a setting in which he may neither move around nor look at his interlocutor. This is thought to be conducive to free association.

By inventing play analysis, Klein gave the child a further means of acting out. The connections that the child makes with his internal objects fluctuate constantly. The child constantly changes level in his mode of relating to his internal objects. The externalisation of the inner world constantly blurs the distinction between internal reality and shared reality. According to Meltzer, the handling of the acting out constitutes the cornerstone of the analytic process with the child.[6] The more dreams the child presents, the less he tends to act out.

Grinberg has proposed a classification of adult dreams according to their propensity to act out.[7] This system of identification also seems to me to have useful application to children's dreams. Dreams can be divided into two main categories:

- either the dream contributes to a work of elaboration
- or the dream serves to expel psychic material.

With children's and adolescents' dreams, we need to give as much careful consideration to the form and function of the dreaming as to the content of the dream. The form and function of the dream reflect the way in which the ego is organised. The transference and countertransference involve much more than verbal communication. There is a constant unspoken interaction through which the child and the adolescent act on the therapist's mind. When dreams are influenced by acting out, I term them 'active dreams'.

PERSONALITY EMERGES BY EVACUATING IN DREAMS

The primary purpose of *evacuative dreams* is to discharge feelings, unconscious phantasies or object relations into an interlocutor. Acting out in waking life is not always adequate to rid the psyche of its intolerable sensations and emotions. It continues in the night in the form of active dreams. Conversely, acting out sometimes completes during the daytime an evacuation that began in the dream. It is sometimes impossible to understand a child's strange behaviour unless he is allowed to talk about the nocturnal dream that he has needed to act out in the daytime.

Justin

Before coming to see me, Justin's mother had tried consultations with two psychologists, a man and a woman, and with a child psychiatrist. As I was working in the same centre as them, I had guessed that she wanted me to say the opposite to my colleague. This colleague had not refrained from saying that her son was delusional and that he needed neuroleptic medication. What was to some extent a dialogue of the deaf between us had begun fairly well. The very most that his mother would concede was that Justin's own parents found him 'very dreamy'. The child, who was coming up to eight years old, had not struck me as frankly psychotic but I had observed several personality defects.

At the second session, I was able to establish better contact with Justin. He agreed to talk to me about the second nightmare of his life because the first had vanished from his memory. 'I am kicking the witch in the backside.' He had told his last dream on condition that I did not breathe a word about it to his mother. 'Mum was dead.' Slightly disconcerted, I indicated that I would like to know more about it. Justin added: 'She sped away in the car and she fell into the sea. (And you?) This was before we were born.' (Justin had a younger brother.)[8]

I sometimes found what Justin said both incoherent and bizarre. He still seemed to have full use of his intelligence. But he was refusing to learn anything at school. He mainly drew violent and brutal heroes from the Japanese cartoons that he was constantly watching on television. I sometimes felt uneasy when he was playing in front of me. When I handed him a small figure that represented one of his favourite cartoon characters, he made it cross the sea and land in an earthquake that overturned all the toys. Then some crystal balls exploded all around him. I repeated my questions in vain; I obtained very few answers. It was as if Justin had been having a nightmare all alone, totally cut off from the external reality of which I was a part.

ELABORATION CAN OCCUR
LONG AFTER AN EVACUATION IN A DREAM

Julie

We are going to look at another case that contained a psychotic dimension, in which it nevertheless became possible to address the dream experience. The mother had brought Julie to see me when she was eight years old for an ordinary reason: her daughter was being disruptive in class and was having difficulty concentrating. It had soon become clear that Julie still felt a strong attachment to her mother. The trouble that Julie had had tolerating the birth of a sister had only intensified this attachment. At this time, Julie, who was over three years old, had just started at nursery school. Also, the family had recently moved house.

What was more unusual here was that Julie had spent some time in hospital when she was four years old because she had had some hallucinations and been delusional. The episode had begun with a sleepless night. The following night, Julie had been afraid of almost everything around her. In the paediatric unit, she refused to let go of her mother and clung on to her. She had been given some neuroleptic medication. The hospital unit had tried to arrange some follow-up care. However, this had soon foundered because of the mother's aloofness and lack of understanding. She had, however, wondered if the eczema that appeared at this time might be a sequel to the psychic decompensation.

Julie had been unstable since starting at nursery school. This had only increased over the years. The parents had felt obliged to consult a psychologist after she started at primary school, but this had soon been cut short. I felt that Julie wanted to come to see me. I asked her if she was having any dreams. No, she was having very few if any at all. She finally told me something that had happened to her one day, but she was still wondering if this had really happened to her. She had been on the ground floor in their house with her elder brother when some burglars had arrived. The parents had gone down to the cellar to fetch a bottle of wine. The burglars had gone upstairs while she and her brother were hiding under the table. A large wasp had appeared. Julie was so convinced that this had really happened that she was disappointed when her mother said otherwise.

Some time later, Julie told me about another nightmare. As she had a poor sense of time, it was impossible to know if it was recent or old. 'There was a witch. She had a stomach in place of her head and her head was where her stomach should be. The result was a large mouth in the middle of her stomach. One day, she came to the house. We were sleeping outside. We were camping out. It is a dream! I shouted when she arrived. Mum and Dad got up. She ate first them, then my sister. My brother and I ran away. We found each other behind a tractor. She did not see us. She went into another house. I forgot to say: Victor was on a skateboard and I had skates on.'

I encouraged Julie to draw the witch after we had talked a bit about the witch-puppet. Julie was surprised to find a Medusa head or an enormous sun because the 'legs' below multiplied to fill the whole picture. A few weeks later, Julie had wanted to draw Mickey Mouse. She had insisted on knowing what colour my trousers were before drawing these for this character. Julie confirmed that she wanted to go on seeing me. The conversations became easier.

Julie surprised me by announcing that she remembered the 'nightmare' from her stay in hospital. 'I was surrounded by dinosaurs. There was one large one and two small ones. (Julie agreed to draw them.) They wanted to eat me. Near them, there were two more dinosaurs a bit further away. I managed to pass between them. I was very frightened. I ran away. I saw a house. In the house, there were some people with two faces: red and purple, yellow and pink. (I pointed out to Julie that she was wearing yellow and pink.) I opened the door. I quickly shut it again as soon as I saw them. I ran away.'

JULIE

Julie explained to me that she had come back home after her stay in hospital. 'But, there too, I was afraid when I opened my eyes because the dream was still there.' Finally, Julie wanted to draw my portrait. I posed for her. She said that she would not draw my glasses. The result was not very flattering because she had associated my face with a television series that frightened her.

JULIE

There is also the extreme case of *prophetic dreams*.[9] This type of dream appears to predict an event because it automatically causes it to be acted out. Its deficient elaboration gives rise to a scenario in which it is acted out in waking life. Prophetic dreams have certain identifying characteristics: a relatively crude expression, the impression of a concrete experience, the attenuation of internal–external boundaries and a tendency to expel mental contents. These are precisely the same characteristics that we use to describe mental manifestations in children who are bordering on psychosis.

ELABORATIVE DREAMS CAN HELP
TO RESOLVE PSYCHIC CONFLICTS

Unlike evacuative dreams, *elaborative dreams* have a capacity for transformation. Dreaming thus becomes a primary form of preconscious thought. It provides a way of focusing on events that may have been more important than they were thought to be. It has a certain creative power. Psychoanalysis established its dream theory on the basis of elaborative dreams. This theory was informed by Freud's self-analysis, as someone with a neurotic structure, in mid-life, at the height of his dreaming capacities. It is different for the vast majority of people and, especially, for children and adolescents.

Most dreams are situated between the two extremes of evacuation and elaboration. These are *mixed dreams*, which oscillate between remembering and acting out. They instigate compromises in order to preserve representations that have been excluded from memory by the compulsion towards identical repetition. In other words, both the form and the content of the dream have to be addressed with children and adolescents. We begin by discovering the function that the dream fulfils in relational life if its content eludes conscious thought. We are now going to consider some examples of dreams that are more or less mixed at different times.

Romain

Romain was referred to me by a paediatrician. He had been experiencing such severe headaches and stomach pains that his mother had frequently been called by the school. She had decided to take him to a paediatric hospital. All the tests had been conducted, including with the scanner. Nothing had been found to be physically wrong with him. The mother and son had waited four months before following the paediatrician's advice. We met just as Romain was about to start his fourth year of secondary school.

His mother had located the origin of his difficulties in a remote period of his life. Romain had contracted meningitis immediately after he was born. Romain himself had rejected this explanation and mentioned all the cases of cancer from which members of his family had suffered. Romain had only known his mother's family. She had confirmed this: 'I have been alone since the fifth month of the pregnancy.'

Romain had very quickly shown some scepticism as to what I might be able to do for him. Since his headaches had been termed 'imaginary', he felt there was nothing that I could do. He had nevertheless told me a dream. He was in the housing estate in which he lived. The doors were shut. A flying saucer had appeared over it. He had hidden in an empty flat, near the tennis court. He had seen some extra-terrestrials come down. He was keen on science fiction.

Romain believed in extra-terrestrials in an ostensibly rational way. He remembered an incident that had occurred when he was three years old. He and his mother had been staying at his grandparents' house. He had got up in the night. He had noticed that his shadow, projected on the ground and the wall, was glowing. It had come alive and been transformed into a supernatural being. He had called people over to tell them about his discovery but they had not believed him.

The next time, Romain had told me that his headaches had diminished, despite having started back at school a few days earlier. I had understood that this improvement was nothing to do with me. His mother had taken him to an osteopath, who had mobilised his body. This had also awakened some valuable childhood memories.

At the age of six years, Romain had broken his arm in a fall. 'I was being fairly unbearable. I was running all over the house because I was bored. My mother and grandfather were watching telly. They asked me to go and play outside. I climbed on to the garage roof. There was a cat there. I ran after it. I crossed over the transparent sheeting. I scraped my hands as I tried to hold on. I finally let go and fell down. I saw a picture before I crashed on to the ground. I put my hand out. Everything went blank. I woke up when someone creaked open the garage door.'

Romain had had nightmares on the nights that followed. The vision of the picture was frightening him. As he fell, he had caught sight of a large picture that one of his mother's sisters had left in the garage. It was a man with a large white beard. Romain suddenly wondered if the bright shadow that had frightened him before might have been the man in the picture. No, that was impossible. The vision must have taken place after the accident.

Romain remembered that he had done a drawing of what he had seen while he was falling. I asked him if he could draw this again for me. He hesitated, saying that he could not draw well. He began by drawing the back view of a young child. It was himself looking at something. Opposite him, Romain drew the various garage doors. On the other side of the paper, he drew the figure. I pointed out to him that he could draw well, almost to a professional standard. He had in fact confided to me that he was planning to become a cartoonist.

Romain then decided to make the face bigger and put it in the middle of the paper. 'The gaze frightens me. It was very cold. With brown eyes.' I helped him to associate to this. He thought of a Tintin book called *Cigars of the Pharaoh*. There is a portrait gallery in the castle at Moulinsart. A man with a large white beard shuts himself in the coffin with Tintin. He went mad because he was being drugged. Similarly, Romain said that people would think he was mad if he talked about his vision.

The next time, Romain confirmed that there was something that he still remembered extremely well from his childhood. This was a detail of the picture in the dream. The man was sitting at a desk. He was leaning on it to write a letter. I was struck by the similarity with me, as I was in the process of recording the dream as I leant on my desk. But no, there was no connection with this. Besides, the whole picture was dark on a green background.

Part Two
How Do Children Dream?

5
Dreams in the Laboratory

I have thus far considered dreams from a psychoanalytic perspective. I shall next be examining how dreaming has become a field of investigation within neurophysiology. A few skirmishes apart, a relatively peaceful coexistence has been established between neurophysiology and psychoanalysis. By way of illustration, here is the interesting definition given by the official representatives of the American Psychoanalytical Association: 'Dreaming, dreams: Dreaming is a universal and normal, regressive, psychophysiological phenomenon occurring periodically during sleep in regular cycles about ninety minutes apart. Rapid eye movements (REM), which occur in stage 1 of sleep, indicate dreaming.'[1]

If we compare the two periods of 1900 and 1950, a paradigm shift seems to have taken place.[2] The invention of psychoanalysis revolutionised the interpretation of dreams. The dreamer provides associations that, animated by the transference, ultimately retrace the steps by which the dream has been constituted. With the emergence of neurophysiology, an objective and experimental approach to dream processes has overshadowed the interpretation of its contents. So successful has this approach proved that numerous published works have sought to marry the findings of the two disciplines. Some psychoanalysts have even trained as neurophysiologists, working both in the consulting room and in the laboratory.

The new 'paradigm' sought to establish that the dream was nothing more than paradoxical sleep. A near consensus emerged around the hypothesis that rapid-eye-movement (REM) sleep (or paradoxical sleep) is the physiological substratum of the oneiric function, although this has never been conclusively proven. With many others, I maintain that paradoxical sleep should not be conflated with the psychological dream.

In the 1980s, dream research gained a new inspiration with the emergence of a cognitivist approach, alongside psychoanalysis and neurophysiology. The emphasis moved yet further away from the dream, the end product, to dreaming, the process of production. A longitudinal study was conducted on children's dreams in order to cover everything that occurred from childhood to adolescence.[3] *It emerged that dreaming is not a capacity that is immediately acquired but the outcome of a long process that occurs in parallel with mental development in waking life.*

Substantial differences were found between the dreams obtained in the laboratory and those recorded by the parents at home. When the child slept at home, he would remember a dream, on average, every other night. If the same child spent the night in the laboratory, he would manage, on average, to remember two dreams from three awakenings during paradoxical sleep.

Most of our dreams either do not enter our waking consciousness or are completely forgotten.

Children remember their dreams selectively. The reasons for this are still completely open to debate: does the laboratory environment cause a mental inhibition or does the home environment operate a bias on our memory? The child makes choices according to the context. Reference was made to the sleep of the foetus and the newborn baby, who experience the most different conditions from those of the adult. The substantial proportion of sleep in life and the high percentage of paradoxical sleep were still strikingly apparent. Paradoxical sleep may be the primitive matrix of thought, since it allows a hallucinatory resumption of lived experiences and reflective thought.

THE PSYCHOLOGICAL DREAM DIFFERS FROM PARADOXICAL SLEEP

Paradoxical sleep should not be confused with the psychological dream. A brain function has enabled the latter to become a cultural datum. Its basis in paradoxical sleep has been the source of a great developmental potential. Primary mentalisation, with its essential symbolising capacity, requires intermittent operational support from brain productions, with an essentially visual component.

Solms recently considered the question in relation to patients suffering from neurosurgical lesions.[4] He studied those who complained of specific changes in their dreams and who traced these changes back to the onset of their illness. He established a distinction between REM sleep, defined by purely physiological criteria, and dreaming as a psychological process. These two phenomena occur simultaneously, but it does not follow that they are one and the same thing.

Solms made a two-fold discovery. He ascertained that patients with lesions of the brain stem continued to dream. This was a completely unexpected finding because the neurophysiology of dreams assumed an anatomico-physiological correlation between REM sleep and a specific region of the brain stem. Moreover, some other patients with parietal frontal lesions no longer dreamed at all. Solms concluded from this that the structures of the forebrain are essential for dreaming but that the brain stem structures are not.

Solms regards his neurological work as a striking confirmation of Freud's dream theory. I will qualify his conclusion. The fundamental process of paradoxical sleep is indeed located in the brain stem. Psychological dreaming based on the recent (frontal and parieto-occipital) brain structures has arisen and evolved from this physiological oneiric activity. Accordingly, the dream as such – namely, the symbolic functions, spatial orientation, visual representation and affect regulation – is based on the operation of these structures.

DREAMING IS A MENTAL ACTIVITY DURING SLEEP

'Our early conviction was that REM sleep and dreaming were exactly synonymous and that NREM sleep was a mental void – an oblivion.'[5] It was found that dream memories could also be obtained when subjects awoke during slow sleep. As this did not often occur, it was thought to involve persistent memories originating from an earlier paradoxical phase. However, it had to be accepted that dream memories could develop in the first period of slow sleep before any paradoxical sleep had manifested itself.

The dream reports obtained in the laboratory were examined in closer detail and wide variations were found. It was essential to determine which types of report could be accepted as a dream and which could not.[6] First of all, everyone has dreams. The nature of the dream reminds us of Saint Augustine's observation about time: 'What, then, is time? If no one ask of me, I know; if I wish to explain to him who asks, I know not.'[7]

What we learn to designate as a 'dream' depends not only on the subjective experiences that we have during sleep but more particularly on the way in which we and those around us have reflected on it after waking up. In 1962, Foulkes was the first to make a study of mental activity during NREM (non-rapid-eye-movement) sleep.[8] This marked the transition from neurophysiology to cognitivist psychology.

This led to a slightly different viewpoint. Dreaming is no longer synonymous with REM sleep, but we dream more easily during paradoxical sleep. The latter is neither a necessary nor a sufficient condition for dream production. Foulkes asked the volunteers to describe everything that came into their minds rather than to say what they had dreamt. He accepted as a response anything that revealed mental activity, including what we might call 'thought narratives'.

Cognitivist psychology distinguished the production of the dream from its memorisation. The dream depends on complex cognitive processes that process information stored in the memory. It became possible to separate the production of the dream during sleep and its restitution in speech after waking.[9] Similarly, psychoanalysts who also conducted neurophysiological research differentiated between activation of the memory and processing the information and between the type of thought and its formulation into a narrative.

THE CHILD NEEDS SYMBOLIC ACTIVITY TO DREAM

With children, there has been little systematic research linking the collection of dream reports with their encephalographic recordings. Foulkes conducted a longitudinal study that has become a major reference-point.[10] He obtained the dream reports in the laboratory after having awoken some children on nine nights over a five-year period. One group consisted of children aged from three to nine years old and another consisted of nine- to fifteen-year-old children. The first group was the more interesting of the two because children change a great deal during this period and their dreams also develop considerably.

As we have noted, Foulkes was a cognitivist psychologist. He expanded the definition of the dream report by considering dreams produced during NREM sleep. For him, 'dreams themselves *are* mental acts'.[11] Dreaming is closer to thought than to vision. Children show in their dreams how they can represent and organise what happens in their lives. They can tell us how they think about themselves, others and the external world.

Piaget has been criticised by researchers who followed him. For Foulkes, however, Piaget's schema for the development of representational intelligence remained entirely apposite. Concerning dreams, the critical turning-point occurs when the child becomes capable of truly symbolic activity. He is able clearly to show his capacity to represent an object that has long since disappeared. This occurs in the second half of the second year of life (between around eighteen and twenty-four months).

Foulkes took up the five manifestations that appear at this point, for their simultaneous presence signals the onset of symbolic activity:

- deferred imitation: the child repeats what he has observed – for example, tapping his foot in imitation of the anger shown earlier by a young friend;
- verbal reference to past events: the child says: 'Daddy gone', pointing his finger in the direction in which the man went;
- drawings (or other artistic reproductions) of absent objects or events;
- behaviours that seem to be generated by mental imagery, including absent objects;
- symbolic play: the child knows how to pretend; for example, miming a steam train operating at full throttle.

YOUNG CHILDREN REPORT
LESS DREAM MATERIAL IN THE LABORATORY

Foulkes found in his longitudinal study that dreaming was dictated more by intellectual development than by perceptual skills: 'It seems to be how children are able to think, rather than how or what they are able to sense or see, that determines the form and substance of their dreams.'[12] The first age group, from three to five years old, corresponds to the pre-operational phase. Foulkes first observed that the children reported very few dreams when awoken during REM sleep and that they reported less material. Just over one quarter of the awakenings gave rise to an account containing fourteen words on average (none contained more than fifty words).

A second observation related to the major differences between what was reported by children as opposed to adults. The children's accounts did not involve someone in the process of doing something, people they knew, strangers, feelings or human interactions. Given such deficiencies, the question arose as to what in fact remained: themes revolving around bodily states (hunger, sleep) and almost immobile animals. One child 'sees himself' sleeping in the bath instead of his bed; another 'sees' hens pecking at grain.

Foulkes concluded from these reports that three- to five-year-old children are primarily interested in animals. He pointed out that it is no coincidence that stories and cartoons for children mainly involve animal characters. The dreams feature animals that are neither very familiar or individualised, nor exotic or frightening. The animals that appear are usually farm animals or animals from the immediate natural world (birds, deer, frogs and so on) but not dangerous animals.

Foulkes thought that these animals lent themselves best to projective identification. As he never shrank from controversy, he emphasised the absence of frightening images (ogres, demons), acts of aggression and emotions. All this runs counter to psychoanalytic theories, which attribute complicated and violent emotions to young children. It is clear that Foulkes' descriptions differ substantially from those of Despert (examined in Part One). My own experience accords more with Despert's observations.

Foulkes wondered if there was not nevertheless a common factor in the dreams of young children and those of adults. They all constitute 'a creative recombination of memories and knowledge'.[13] In this sense, even young children are capable of dreaming; this goes beyond remembering isolated fragments of events they have experienced and reproducing a previous recording – dreaming as action replay.

OLDER CHILDREN REPORT MORE DREAM MATERIAL

Foulkes studied the same children two years later. They did not report many more dreams at five to seven years than at three to five years of age. However, their reports were significantly longer, increasing from fourteen to forty-one words on average. The most striking changes, however, related to the contents. The number of physical movements (particularly journeys) substantially increased. The representation of physical states was replaced by the representation of human interactions. Human beings had come to occupy the same position of importance as animals. Some stories evolved through a sequence of interconnected events. Finally, they featured characters that were totally invented or unknown to the child in waking life.

Several aspects of adults' dreams obtained in the same conditions were not found. The reports were still shorter. They were not truly structured as narratives. The dreamer did not always represent himself as an active participant. This was accompanied by a relative absence of emotions. There was much social interaction but the dreamer did not take part in it. It should be noted that all the children in the study were at school by this stage. They were probably learning how to respond to the requests of adults other than their parents. However, this had not helped them to describe their dreams and represent themselves in these.

The same group of children was studied two years later. They were now seven to nine years old. There were some changes in the amount of material. The proportion of reports obtained from awakenings had risen from one third to approximately one half. The reports had also continued to increase in length – from forty-one to sixty-three words on average. Some qualitative changes were also observed. As regards the narrative quality, the children were abandoning stories consisting only of a sequence of events in favour of stories unified by a general theme or plot. Another change related to the dreamer's increasing presence and participation. This coincided with a reduction in dreams about animals. This last change was due to the emergence of thoughts and feelings attributed to the characters in the dream.

From this point onwards, dreaming took place on both a psychological and a physical level. Interestingly, the most frequent emotion to appear was happiness. In general, it was the dreamer who was happy. If they were not radiantly happy, the characters were engaged in friendly social interaction. It may be surprising to find that happiness is the earliest human emotion and that which is most easily identifiable in children of that age. Foulkes did not neglect to restate his belief: the development of children's dreaming can be predicted based on what we know about their mental development in waking life.

Between the ages of nine and thirteen years, the development of the dreaming capacity begins to peak. The child approaches the adult's achievements in terms of the percentage and the length of reports. The dreamer is represented as much as other people are. There is a greater variety of emotions. Fear and anger then emerge in dreams. Physical activities and social interactions become more realistic. Finally, dreams reflect the interests and behaviour of waking life even more closely.

Finally, Foulkes raised the question of gender difference. The reader may have noticed that the dreamer's sex has not yet been considered. If behaviour in waking life reappears in dreams, there should have been observable differences between the dreams of boys and girls. Foulkes skilfully adduced the knowledge that boys and girls acquired concerning gender roles. The main difference seems to be that children are more interested in children of the same sex as themselves than in those of the opposite sex. In short, boys dream more about boys and girls more about girls.

Foulkes conceded that young people moved away from this pattern from the age of thirteen years. Girls' dreams then demonstrated less aggressive forms of behaviour. Later, these same dreams revealed the tendency to maintain stronger family ties and an attachment to the home. We should probably bear in mind that Foulkes' study dates from the 1970s and that customs, particularly in sexual behaviour, have changed considerably since that period.

DO CHILDREN HAVE THE SAME DREAMS IN THE LABORATORY AS AT HOME?

Foulkes had anticipated some criticisms of his method of studying children's dreams. For example, does sleeping in a laboratory affect how children dream? Can repeated observation influence the answers the children give after waking up? Foulkes decided to set up some control groups. In 1979, he published a comparative study of laboratory dreams and dreams at home.[14]

Research conducted among adults had already established the contrast between dreams obtained in the laboratory by waking the dreamer and those that the dreamer remembered spontaneously on waking. In the first instance, the typical dream is relatively insignificant and commonplace. It resembles what happens in daily life. In the second instance, the dream often contains a fantastical plot and intense and unpleasant emotions. A study conducted with young adults did not find striking differences between laboratory dreams and dreams at home. However, more physical and verbal aggression appeared in dreams at home. It would seem that the laboratory environment either reduces the expression of aggressive impulses or reinforces the inhibition of aggression.

Two hypotheses have been suggested to account for these differences:

- either the subjects are too inhibited in the laboratory to allow themselves to have or to relate dream experiences because the context intensifies the awareness of what is happening internally;
- or the subjects who dream at home are operating an important form of selection. They are remembering only the most striking or the most disturbing dreams.

DREAMING IS AN ELEMENTARY
BUT PRIMORDIAL FORM OF THOUGHT

The normal gestation period for a human female is forty weeks. At the beginning, there is an observable increase in the amount of active sleep.[15] This proportion rises from 45% to 65% of the period of total sleep between thirty-two and thirty-six weeks. This amount begins to diminish slightly before the end of the gestation period.

This large amount of active or seismic sleep occurs in all mammals that, like the human being, are born with an undeveloped nervous system. The development of sleep and brain activity depend on the age of conception. For example, a premature baby born after six months of pregnancy will sleep in a similar way at the age of three months to a baby born at term.

Paradoxical sleep diminishes considerably and rapidly during the first two years of life. At six months, it represents no more than 30% of the total period of sleep. At the age of one year, the baby falls asleep in slow sleep, like an adult. From the age of two years, the amount of paradoxical sleep is close to that of the young adult. It has been asked why there is so much active sleep at six months of pregnancy, why it diminishes so fast and whether active sleep can be considered as an equivalent of paradoxical sleep.[16]

This diminution does not seem to result from the development of the cortex, which has an inhibiting effect on the stimuli that originate from the brain stem, but simply to show that the paradoxical sleep has fulfilled its primitive functions. This has been the source of much speculation. Paradoxical sleep has been thought to be involved in the child's neural and cognitive development. The best-known and the most interesting theory was put forward by Roffwarg, who suggested that endogenous stimulation plays a vital role during gestation and after birth; that is, before exogenous stimulation comes to predominate.[17]

Another interesting view is put forward by Debru, who interprets this more freely.[18] The newborn baby can be conditioned. Accordingly, active sleep enables him to integrate the different sensory modes of foetal experience. Paradoxical sleep may be the primitive matrix of thought to the extent that it allows a hallucinatory resumption of lived experience. It thus provides a basis for what will become the reflective function.

6

Can Blind Children Dream
Without the Use of Their Eyes?

Children who are blind from birth have attracted the interest of researchers because they are thought to provide an opportunity for considering sightlessness in an almost experimental way. It has been asked whether it is possible to dream without seeing and, if so, what in fact can be 'seen' in this condition. Sighted people have therefore reflected on what blindness might be like by imagining being blind. This accords with the realm of fantasies and myths. Researchers have also been intrigued by the fact that a high percentage of congenitally blind people bear resemblances with sighted children who have become autistic. Some have considered autists to be suffering from 'mental blindness'. This raises some questions about the role of sight in mental development.

The blind child cannot be considered simply as an ordinary child who cannot see. The situation is more complex than this because the missing sensory functions can be compensated by the other senses and an integration of perceptions and sensations can be established from the outset in an intermodal way. The nature of the problem changes if we accept that the role of sight is substituted by the role of language in blind children.

THE PHILOSOPHER PRETENDS TO PUT OUT HIS EYES
SO AS TO GAIN A BETTER UNDERSTANDING OF SIGHT

Diderot wrote a 'Letter on the blind for the use of those who see'.[1] He examined some beliefs attributed to blind people in order to expound a materialist and atheistic view of the universe. Idealism could have been conceived by blind people because idealists are philosophers who are aware only of their existence and a series of internal sensations. According to the idealist viewpoint, like blind people, we never emerge from inside ourselves and we only perceive our own thought.

Diderot concludes his essay by discussing a problem posed by Molyneux, a 17th-century English physician. This problem has been the subject of numerous controversies. Let us imagine someone blind from birth who has learnt to distinguish by touch a cube from a sphere, which are made of the same metal and approximately the same size. Then we suppose that this blind person acquires the capacity to see. Would he be able to distinguish the cube from the sphere if he saw them without touching them?

Diderot addressed the problem because in the mid-18th century some congenitally blind people were having their sight restored through cataract operations. He stated that it was for the philosopher rather than the natural scientist to put questions to blind people who had regained their sight. 'I would have less confidence in the impressions of a person seeing for the first time than in the discoveries of a philosopher who had profoundly meditated on the subject in the dark; or, to adopt the language of the poets, who had put out his eyes in order to be the better acquainted with vision.'[2] At the unconscious level, the famous philosopher was not immune to the fantasies of sighted people who try to put themselves in the shoes of the blind.

According to some stories, Athene blinded Tiresias because he had inadvertently glimpsed the naked goddess bathing. Tiresias' mother managed to appeal to the goddess, who agreed to give him an understanding of the language of prophecy in recompense. Other versions of the myth relate that one evening Tiresias saw two snakes mating. The snakes wanted to attack him. He killed the female snake and in punishment for this he was turned into a woman who became a prostitute. Seven years later, he witnessed the same scene in the same place. He became a man again by killing the male snake.

Diderot used rational enquiry to question an intelligent man who was born blind. Diderot asked him what he understood by mirror. The blind person only knows objects through touch, whereas others know them by sight. The blind man concluded that sight must be a form of touch that apprehends distant objects. Since touch incorporates a concept of relief, a mirror must be a device that throws us into relief in the world beyond us. Winnicott has argued persuasively that the mother's face constitutes a precursor of the mirror. The blind person must therefore have great difficulty in representing to himself his own psychic life and that of others. Diderot did not address the question of dreams but he denied any imagination to the congenitally blind person, whom he thought would relate everything to the extremity of his fingers.

'We combine coloured points, he only palpable points, or, to speak more precisely, only such tactile sensations as he remembers ... he does not create an image, for to do this it is necessary to colour a background and mark upon it points of a different colour from that background. Make these points of the same colour as the ground, and they are at once lost in it, and the figure disappears.' Diderot cautiously added: 'at any rate, that is the case in my imagination'.[3]

Little has changed in two centuries, since most studies devoted to congenitally blind people start from the premise that they are identical to sighted people apart from being unable to see. An American reference work listed over 300 studies of the early development of blind children in the 1980s.[4] These works all promote the idea that visual impairment does not in itself cause any developmental delay or deficiency. However, blind children have more trials and obstacles to overcome as they grow up.[5] They have been an object of study both for neurologists and for psychoanalysts.

CONGENITALLY BLIND PEOPLE DO NOT SCAN WITH THEIR GAZE

Some laboratory research was conducted into congenitally blind people at the beginning of the 1960s in relation to the 'scanning hypothesis'. When rapid eye movements were discovered, they were thought to be connected with dream images. In other words, the eyes move because they are following the images in the dream. They follow the action that is unfolding in the scene of the dream or at the very least they glance towards it.

It was hypothesised that precisely the same activities occur in the brain during paradoxical sleep as in the waking state. In other words, the dreamer believes in the reality of the dream because the brain processes the sensory impulses in the same way whether it is dreaming or awake. Confirmation of this was sought from congenitally blind subjects. It was thought that because their dreams did not contain visual images, they would not 'scan' with their eyes during paradoxical sleep.

The hypothesis was at first supported by the discovery that the eyes move a great deal in active dreams, whereas they are hardly mobilised at all in passive dreams. An attempt was made to demonstrate that the eye muscles behave during paradoxical sleep as if they were receiving identical information to that in the waking state. At first, a strong correlation was found between the eye movements recorded by a researcher and the reconstitution of these movements based on dream reports by another researcher who was working independently of him.

A group of congenitally blind people initially provided confirmation of the absence of eye movements among them. However, they would tell dreams when they were woken during the paradoxical phase. Other experiments obtained completely contradictory results and the research became embroiled in methodological controversies. The reverse hypothesis was put forward: instead of being the consequence of dream imagery, eye movements contribute to the neurophysiological processes that generate this imagery. It was also thought that eye movements and visual images were produced in parallel but independently by the same generator. Laboratory studies of blind people were abandoned and the scanning hypothesis was shelved.

HOW DO BLIND CHILDREN DREAM?

Peter

Fraiberg conducted an extensive observation of a blind child with arrested development.[6] Peter received therapy from her in his own home between the ages of nine and eleven years. This was a highly instructive case because his mother began an analysis a few months after her son's treatment started. Peter was making slow progress in terms of separation and identification. His boundaries between himself and other people had not stabilised. They could easily become blurred or disappear temporarily.

Fraiberg mentioned dreams only once. At the end of the second year of treatment, Peter was better able to distinguish himself from his mother and to talk about things that frightened him. "'What woke you up last night, Peter?" "I had a dream." "Tell me a story about the dream." "The garage was all gone.""[7] The therapist was not surprised by this because she had learnt that the garage had in fact been knocked down the day before the dream in order to enlarge the garden.

Fraiberg thought that Peter did not want to go to sleep because he preferred to avoid being disturbed by a dream. He was in the habit of going to sleep while holding his favourite sea-shell. If he woke up in the night and could not find it, he was unable to settle down until he was holding it again. Fraiberg inferred from this that one of the reasons for not going to bed came from the fear of losing his identity while he was asleep.

There is only one publication about dreams in visually impaired people.[8] It was written by a psychologist who was congenitally blind. Buquet set out to challenge the assertion that visual material predominates in dream scenarios. There is no doubt that blind people have dreams. But what are their dreams like? Do they feel that anything is deficient or lacking in relation to sight? Their dreams contain objects, but these are apprehended in the same way as in waking life. They are masses and forms that are felt mentally. The blind person dreams with his representation of reality, which is radically different from that of the sighted person.

Buquet has discussed the role played by representations originating from the various senses:

- Taste is often associated with touch. For example, a bad-tasting substance, chewed or spat out, may express horror and expulsion.
- Hearing: voices are deeper than usual. These can be penetrating or paralysing. They can give orders that convey taboo or prohibition.
- Touch is used across an entire spectrum: from a light brush to a deep bite. Interlocutors may float alongside or glide over the dreamer. Touch can be associated with hearing: a wrenching sensation may be accompanied by a noise. Tactility can be combined with synaesthesia: a cold sensation can inform the dreamer that he is sleeping naked.

The author provided only one child's dream. An eight-year-old girl dreams that she is climbing up an almost vertical slope with her childhood friend, who is also blind. She has to make considerable effort to move herself up the slope. She finally reaches the summit. She is overjoyed to find that she is walking barefoot on a velvet carpet. The joy rises from her feet to her head. She feels as if she is in heaven. She concludes that she will not be able to stay in this wonderful place without undergoing some preliminary trial.

A terrifying character sets her down on her hands and knees. He energetically rubs her back with a hard brush, but the bristles do not hurt her very much. She then has the right to stay in this wonderful place. She is happy to find that the punishment was not as terrible as she had anticipated. In telling the dream, she remembered that she was given injections every week from the age of two years old. She had not always liked this and she had to be held still for it to be done. This is a scenario that might appear in a sighted girl's dream. But the dream is different in that sensation takes the place of the visual image. The sensation of movement combines with the cutaneous sensation to convey the body's relationship with the environment.

SIGHTLESSNESS IMPEDES PERSONALITY DEVELOPMENT

Blindness at an early age is a relatively rare affliction in the industrialised world. This is fortunate because it has a strong impact on the child and on those around him. Sight has been accorded an important role in acquiring knowledge and adapting to the social environment. An attempt was made to regard childhood blindness as a form of experimental setting by considering the blind child as a child deprived of one of the five senses. Studying blind children would thus provide a way of assessing the role of vision in the development of sighted children.[9]

An average mother spontaneously provides her baby with two complementary functions: providing stimuli and protecting from them. When the baby is blind from birth, the mother manages to compensate for the handicap by familiarising him with olfactory and gustatory, and particularly tactile and auditory, sensations. However, this same mother also gives protection by filtering stimuli and removing those that are too strong.

Blindness does not constitute in itself an impediment to development. For example, the effects of blindness can be attenuated by appropriate educational measures. Unfortunately, the revelation of a serious handicap can cause a traumatic neurosis in the parents, in particular the mother. Consequently, there is a risk that the mother's discourse will relate everything that goes badly to the child's blindness and to the external world.[10]

Fraiberg studied ego development in congenitally blind people. She was intrigued by the relatively high incidence of ego disorders in the congenitally blind because they resembled the clinical profile of autism in sighted children.[11] This profile also includes some other symptoms; for example, the hands do not seem to have any autonomy in relation to the mouth. Sightlessness is not an adequate explanation for these disturbances because many congenitally blind children manage to attain a similar degree of ego integration to that achieved by sighted children. Abnormal blind children exhibit arrested development in relation to a primary and undifferentiated mouth. All this seems to point to the existence of a critical period between nine and eighteen months of age.

Theories of ego development are implicitly based on the role of sight. Sighted children use vision to structure the other sensory modes. Furthermore, the mother is not the only source of learning from experience. Fraiberg referred to Piaget's theory of the construction of reality. Piaget had demonstrated that sighted children conduct a series of experiments between the ages of nine and eighteen months that lead to the discovery that an object exists even when they can no longer see it. Sighted children manage to rediscover the object in complex situations using visual reconstructions. By contrast, blind children have to trace the object's movements through perceptual clues (for example, sounds) that are much less accessible than those provided by sight. It is the mother, as a strongly cathected person, who helps the blind child to learn about object permanency. He will finally discover that his mother continues to exist when he can no longer touch or hear her.

VISION HELPS WITH FORMING REPRESENTATIONS OF THE WORLD

Blind children use auditory stimuli to identify a bird by its song and to locate it in space. However, they have no notion either of its shape or its size, or of its trajectory. They can describe certain objects that they cannot touch, but they cannot apprehend drawings, stars or colours, or very small or very large objects.

Piaget discovered that the earliest mental categories, such as the concepts of weight, volume and object permanency, originate from a sensory and motor interaction with the surrounding world. Blind children begin the sensorimotor phase in the same way as sighted children. But a certain delay becomes apparent from the age of four months.

Towards the end of the 1970s, the results of several experiments raised some questions concerning how children apprehend the world by connecting their experiences. It was asked how they learn that something that is seen and touched separately can be one and the same thing. How do they manage to coordinate the information that they obtain about a single external source through several senses?

In one experiment, some three-week-old infants were given one or other of two very different dummies to suck. When the blindfolds were removed, it was observed that the infants looked more at the dummy that they had had in their mouths. This finding ran counter to Piaget's theory of how reality is discovered and constructed. According to Piaget, the infant begins by forming a schema of the dummy with his mouth, then another schema with his gaze. It is only afterwards that he manages to coordinate the visual and the tactile schemas. The new experiment led to the conclusion that the child does not need these two preliminary stages and that he has an innate connection between the sensations. It also follows from this that children do not need preliminary experiences to form associative connections between what they have felt and what they have seen.

'Infants thus appear to have an innate general capacity, which can be called *amodal perception*, to take information received in one sensory modality and somehow translate it into another sensory modality ... it involves an encoding into a still mysterious *amodal representation*, which can then be recognized in any of the sensory modes.'[12] The breast thus emerges as a partly integrated experience between the sucked aspect and the seen aspect. The child is programmed to carry out certain forms of integration that generate the sense of self.

According to Stern, scientific observation of young children was revolutionised during the latter decades of the 20th century. This revolution occurred because a method was found of putting questions to babies that they were truly capable of answering. In fact, this was less a case of questions that they knew how to answer than questions to which it was possible to obtain generalisable answers through experimentation.

To answer the question 'What do babies like looking at?', a dummy with an electronic chip was placed in each of their mouths and these dummies were then linked to a slide projector. The babies could see the projected image when they sucked. A three-month-old child can thus learn quickly that he can move on to a new image simply by sucking. He also learns that he must stop sucking when he wants to look at another one. The choice of images provided a way of studying children's visual preferences.

Child development is not a linear process. It occurs in leaps and bounds that lead the child into an increasingly complex experiential world. Stern described the series of five experiential worlds that occur from birth to four years of age. At around four months old, the baby enters what he terms the 'Immediate Social World'. Stern referred to 'the rich choreography between himself and his mother … the subtle moves by which they regulate their flow of feelings'.[13]

I have chosen to investigate what happens after four months of age, since the sighted baby and the blind baby have developed in approximately the same way until then. This is all the more interesting because Stern never envisaged the possibility that blind children had dreams.

BLIND CHILDREN HAVE DIFFICULTY
ENTERING THE IMMEDIATE SOCIAL WORLD

How does the baby's entry into the Immediate Social World take place and what does it involve? He learns what pure psychological interaction consists in, without the variations and complications created by social life. He then learns about the non-verbal foundation of all human relationships, on which language will subsequently be constructed. The only thing that counts is the reciprocal attention exchanged by the baby and the caregiver. This is an intersubjective world 'between us' that is solely concerned with what is happening in the 'here and now'.

Stern established that this particular social world is based on the importance of the face and controlling the gaze. In the baby's eyes, the face becomes the most attractive and fascinating object possible. No child, and subsequently no adult, can become a social entity unless he has first been a physiognomist; that is, unless he knows how to read from the face what that person is experiencing and expressing. The baby is interested in every facial characteristic (curves, symmetries, contrasting colours). However, he is also interested in the face because it reacts to everything he does and because various interactions can be instigated through the face.

The baby enters this particular social world because he has begun to control his gaze. He knows how to determine its direction, object and duration. He can initiate or terminate a facial interaction because this is based on a reciprocal gaze. The latter forms the structure of the interpersonal relationship. The baby begins to realise that he is capable of causing events. He also becomes aware that he is a separate entity from his mother and that she and he do not have the same boundaries.

There have been various conflicting psychological theories about how to establish the point at which the young child becomes capable of differentiating himself from his mother and how this occurs. Stern rejects the theory that the baby remains fused with the mother for an extensive period. He regards the baby as capable at an early stage of identifying invariants; that is, things that do not change or that always go together. Accordingly, the baby can make a distinction between self and others at around the third or fourth month of life.

During this period, which lasts until the age of twelve months, the baby begins to form a rudimentary representation of the world. Distinct entities develop here: himself, his mother and his father, perhaps familiar figures in his environment. Each has his own unique face, eyes, expressions, voice and gestures. All of these factors can exert an influence on each other. If the least of these capacities, particularly to see the face and control the gaze, is delayed or absent, there is a risk that all social interaction will be slower to emerge or be diverted off-course. The refusal to maintain or establish any visual contact is a characteristic of the autistic child. We have observed that many congenitally blind people manifest the same clinical characteristics as autistic sighted children.

7
Night Terrors, Sleepwalking and Nightmares

Approximately one tenth of consultations in general paediatrics are for sleep disorders. It is often the same children who are having difficulty getting to sleep and who are waking up in the night. Medicine for sleep disorders emerged in the 1960s, after correlations were found between dreams and REM sleep. Paediatricians and child psychiatrists were able to make use of sleep laboratories, clinics or units.

A fundamental distinction was established between nightmares, with a physiological basis in paradoxical sleep and belonging in the same category as dreams, and night terrors and sleepwalking, which are thought to be oneiric manifestations that occur during slow sleep. *The existence of mental activities other than dreaming during sleep was thus established.*

NIGHT TERRORS APPEAR TO INTERRUPT CHILDREN'S SLEEP

Night terrors constitute major sleep disturbances. These disturbances are caused by waking up during the deepest phase of sleep.[1] The child's body is activated at these times because muscular tonus is preserved during deep sleep and there is very limited mental activity. Adults also experience these difficulties but they occur predominantly in children. Night terrors can arise as soon as the child's sleep cycle comes to resemble the adult cycle – at around five or six months old. However, they occur with maximum frequency during the third and the fourth year. They are rare after five years of age.

Partial waking in the phase of deep sleep can produce scenes ranging from very mild to highly disturbing. At one end of the scale, the child may toss and turn in bed, move around a little, open his eyes for a moment, and chew or mumble before going back to sleep. Somewhere between the two extremes, a child may be seen sitting up in bed, with a dazed expression. He may look around him without seeing anything, as if he is trying to understand. However, he is not sufficiently awake to become conscious. He finally lies down again. He immediately falls back into the deep sleep that he had not really interrupted.

Night terrors in the true sense of the term produce a disturbing scene. The young sleeper suddenly finds himself partly awake. He sits up abruptly in bed. He begins to cry or even to howl. He tosses and turns in bed. The parents find their child sweating, his heart beating wildly. They are shattered to find that he does not recognise them even though his eyes are wide open. Everything they do to calm him down is to no avail. He seems to be in the throes of inner torment. He nevertheless finally goes back to sleep. He returns to a normal sleep cycle, as if nothing had happened.

The diagnosis of night terrors is sometimes based on conversation with the parents about their older or pre-adolescent child. There may have been times during which he has wailed in the night without troubling anyone around him. These were not severe because he managed to get back to sleep on his own. Clinical examination is usually enough to make the diagnosis. Two elements tend to confirm this: the time of night and the age of the child. These difficulties arise at the beginning of the night (less than three hours after going to bed). Eight- to ten-month-old infants may suffer from night terrors. However, these terrors predominantly afflict children between the ages of two and five years old. They can then lead to sleepwalking.

Adults sometimes manage to communicate the mental content of their night terrors. It is poor and very difficult to express in words. It consists in short fragments without actual scenes. There may be an image of a frightening experience such as drowning, a choking sensation, a never-ending fall or a savage attack.[2]

NIGHT TERRORS CAN BYPASS THE DREAM WORK

The use of the sleep laboratory might lead us to doubt the existence of psychic reality. However, physiological causality should not be allowed to eliminate psychic reality. Night terrors are not without significance. They occur at a period when the child is gaining vast amounts of knowledge, his daily universe is expanding considerably and when he is easily unsettled by family events. As Brazelton observed, 'Night terrors usually appear on the nights that follow a tough or stressful day ... The terrors may be a way of working off the leftover steam from the day.'[3]

Alizée

Here is a fairly recent clinical case in which the young child is having difficulty discharging excess tension originating from a past that has been poorly assimilated by the parents. The final outcome in situations of this kind will vary according to whether the parents have enough mental resources to seek and accept psychological help. Alizée came to the consultation with her mother because of sleeping difficulties. She was just over two years old. For several weeks, she had been waking up in the night, thrashing around, beginning to wail. Her mother would get up and come to see her. Alizée did not recognise her, although her eyes were open. Finally, she would go back to sleep. Her mother remained puzzled because she had tried everything in vain. Their general practitioner had carried out an electroencephalogram to eliminate any possibility of epilepsy, but nothing abnormal had been detected in the test.

The parents had decided to consult a specialist. This specialist found it difficult to imagine how Alizée could resemble a raging little demon. He was dealing with a sweet, pleasant and lively little girl. She could already speak fairly well. She could do jigsaws. She had no trouble separating from her mother to go to the playgroup twice a week. The mother had taken parental leave to care full-time for her first child. The parents seemed to be getting on well. However, the father's work often took him away from home for several days at a time.

The history of the child's development and family events can sometimes shed light on underlying difficulties. The pregnancy had not gone well. The mother had been very anxious because a screening test had not eliminated the possibility of a genetic disorder. She had been prepared to have an abortion, but further tests had shown that the foetus was not abnormal. This had done nothing to alleviate a persistent irrational anxiety.

External reality had only reinforced the fantasies because the birth had been difficult. The mother tended to conflate the image of the real baby, slightly impaired by the test, with the baby of her nightmares. Subsequently, Alizée's appearance should have been enough to reassure the mother. However, she still had misgivings about her child's developmental potential. She set about providing Alizée with intellectual stimulation. Alizée responded to this and developed precociously. This mother may have been depressed after the birth, with the result that her daughter grew tired of providing her with emotional stimulation and showing her that she was really alive.

Alizée would go to considerable pains, sometimes ending in exhaustion, during the daytime to reassure her parents and to be the pretty, intelligent little girl of their dreams. As soon as she lay down, she would fall into a very deep sleep. The maternal reverie was partly lacking for her. She was not able to establish internally a process for producing dream thoughts. She could not dream about what had been unimaginable for her parents during the pregnancy. She could only wake up abruptly. There was a risk of a vicious circle developing because she was deriving a secondary benefit from her sleeping difficulties. She had discovered how much power waking up at night gave her over her parents. Therapy sessions, as an aid to parenthood, can make sense of something that is still a 'nameless dread'.

THE SOMNAMBULANT CHILD IS PRESENTING HIMSELF AS AN UNCONSCIOUS SPECTACLE

Sleepwalking worries the child's parents and immediate circle much more than night terrors. They become afraid that the child will open a window and fall out, or even begin to climb on to the roof to walk. Illustrations for children and cartoons have given us the image of a child (or his animal substitute) moving forward with arms outstretched, in a nightshirt, on the edge of a steep drop. In fact, incidents, particularly accidents, are extremely rare.

The child goes back to sleep at the end of the episode without retaining any memory of it the next day. This is understandable since he has not actually woken up. The child gets up and seems to be looking for something. He walks hesitantly and performs some simple actions. He can obey orders. The parents may be relieved to see him obey and return to bed. Often, the walk does not seem to have any purpose. It is sometimes called wandering or restless roaming. The child sometimes appears to be trying to satisfy a physical need. He may be going to urinate or defaecate somewhere other than the lavatory. He may walk towards the fridge and open it, but without taking anything out or eating from it.

The average episode conforms to the pattern I have just described. At one extreme, there is a mild form, with an episode that consists in nothing more than getting up and going back to bed or even sitting up in bed, as in the night terror. At the other end of the scale, in its severe form, sleepwalking appears to be the result of night terrors. The child appears to be trying to run away from something and to want to escape. If the people around him wake him up, he looks confused and ashamed. He does not understand what has happened to him. He only wants to return to bed and go back to sleep. We should emphasise that this severe form is rare. It seems to occur more frequently in girls with fairly severe personality disorders.

Sleepwalking is fairly common, affecting around 8% of the population (15% on some estimates). It mainly occurs in latency-age children (between six and twelve years of age). The episodes cease shortly after puberty. Sleepwalking may coincide with a change of environment or lifestyle or follow on from a highly emotional or stressful experience. Common sense would suggest that it may be the expression of emotional tensions that have been repressed during the daytime and are released during sleep. Mild forms do not require any treatment. Only the forms associated with neurotic symptoms require special attention.

Leo

Only the child's parents and immediate circle can describe the sleepwalking episode, whereas the sufferer himself is unable to say anything about it. An improvement occurs when the sleepwalking episode is transformed into an active dream. This was the case with Leo and his parents, who came to me for therapy sessions over several years. His parents had brought him to see me because he was still peeing in his bed when he was over seven years old. The enuresis seemed to have been perpetuated by the birth of a younger brother, which had been antecedents of enuresis in both the father and the mother, as well as leading to problems in the parents' families. This had not prevented Leo from developing well. It became obvious to me that he was intelligent and imaginative.

At the first consultation, he had just had his first sleepwalking episode. He had got up in the night. He had hit his face on a piece of furniture while he was walking around with his eyes open. Two years later, the enuresis had not disappeared but it was occurring at very irregular intervals. One day, the father had insisted that Leo tell me his dream. This father was convinced that his own enuresis had disappeared because of his dreams. Leo finally told me a very simple dream with some embarrassment. He had gone to the loo and he had peed. But he had realised when he awoke that he was in his bed and not in the loo.

NIGHTMARES ARE ANXIETY DREAMS

The French word 'cauchemar' has a long history, with origins that have been traced back to the 16th century. During the Renaissance, the word meant a ghost that came to trample on the sleeper. Its English equivalent, 'nightmare', used to refer to a monster or demon with the distressing habit of coming to torment someone in their sleep. According to the current definition, it is a bad dream dominated by anxiety.

Psychoanalytic tradition has long conflated all the child's sudden awakenings during the night under the term '*pavor nocturnus*'. Reference is usually made to the definition provided by Jones in the 1930s.[4] The nightmare has three characteristics:

1. A terrible fear.
2. A sensation of paralysis.
3. An impression of a weight pressing down on the chest (the infamous demon that comes to walk over the recumbent sleeper).

This definition was given for adults' nightmares. It has to be adapted to apply to the bad dreams experienced by children. In the 1960s, Mack defined the child's nightmare as 'an anxiety dream in which fear is of such intense degree as to be experienced as overwhelming by the dreamer and to force at least partial awakening'.[5] According to Hartmann, a psychiatry professor who has extensively studied nightmares in the sleep laboratory, 'True nightmares ... are long, vivid, frightening dreams, which awaken the sleeper and are usually clearly recalled.'[6]

Challamel and Thirion broke with the established view by considering the child's nightmare as the inverse form of the night terror. It is a dream that usually occurs during paradoxical sleep, almost invariably at the end of the night. The child is able to communicate what he has experienced in the form of a story. Although he is frightened, there are few or no physical manifestations. He wakes up completely, he recognises his parents and he seeks reassurance. Finally, he can easily remember what has happened to him. He is then afraid of going back to sleep and being left alone in his bed.

Nightmares are often accompanied by inadequate mentalisation. In any case, they foster mental phobia (especially not thinking about or remembering the nightmare) and/or a psychic paralysis. Those encountered during everyday life bear little resemblance to rich and detailed narratives and subtle analyses. Here are two examples that are representative of the unpublished average account, which consists in a few sentences, without any commentary, and does not stir the imagination of the adult listener.

Armand

Armand, who was five and a half years old, agreed to draw for want of any better suggestion. However, he managed to produce a fairly convincing ghost. In answer to my question, he told me: 'A dragon is attacking me. (How big is it?) Smaller than me. It is biting me. (And you aren't doing anything?) I am kicking it.'

Everyone has frightening dreams in childhood. However, nightmares may indicate the onset of a mental disorder. It is impossible to say when listening to the account of a nightmare if it reflects a temporary adaptational difficulty or indicates a personality disorder. The answer to this question has to take account of the personality of the dreamer and of those around him, as well as any events in the family.

Anaïs

Anaïs was nearly five years old when we first met. I had felt uneasy on encountering both a miniature adult who spoke freely and easily and an incoherent and clumsy little child. I asked her if she was having any dreams; she immediately replied that she had had one the night before. There was a wolf in her bedroom and she was calling her father to chase it away. As we were playing with the plasticine, she asked me to make two wolves: a nice one and a nasty one.

She did not have the patience to wait for a material form of splitting to separate the good one from the bad. She got up from her chair to go over to the window: she wanted to make sure that the wolf was not underneath it. She then asked me to make a big tent and we closed all the openings. She was no longer in danger from the wolf. However, the anxiety continued to gnaw away at her and prompt her to violent behaviour. Anaïs destroyed everything that we had made.

The therapy sessions were nevertheless helpful to this child, who presented a psychotic form of unbalanced development. She managed to portray what was tormenting her in the role play. At one of our last meetings, Anaïs wanted me to act out the dream scene in which the wolf was trying to devour her. As she was not yet capable of make-believe, she actually put out the light in my office in order to make it night. This time, the wolf (whose role had been assigned to me) went past her without seeing her and without managing to find her.

She wanted to reverse the roles. When she became the wolf, she instantly devoured me heartily. She delighted in my agonised groans. We managed to act the same scenario with the mother at the end of the consultation. The mother chose to be the wolf. When the game was over, Anaïs seemed frightened, although she had taken refuge on her mother's lap.

Children do not tend to talk spontaneously about their bad dreams – on the contrary. Many parents are reluctant to listen to them in this way. They ignore or trivialise what they do not want to hear ('It is only a dream, look, have something to drink and go back to sleep'). However, children sometimes retain the memory of a nightmare until adolescence. They may then decide to confide it, according to how far their capacity to contain their emotions, to mentalise, has increased.

Sylvie

I shall now explore the differences in dreaming capacities with reference to another young girl with a more neurotic organisation. Often every possible resource has to be used in a therapy session if the dream is to be formulated in an intelligible way. Sylvie was five years old when she had the dream. She had become potty-trained, both day and night, at the age of two years. But she had started to poo in her pants again at around the age of four. With my help, her mother had remembered that she had had to be away at that time for professional reasons. She had then managed to tell me that she had also had to spend a few weeks in hospital on account of 'nervous depression'.

Sylvie was still torn between her desire to be a girl and to be a boy. She knew that her mother wanted to have another child (probably a boy). She had also discovered that her mother had been away again following a miscarriage. Her mother had exacerbated her jealousy and her envy during the school holidays by looking after a relative's baby (a boy). Sylvie had decided to restrict her food intake in order to avoid becoming pregnant. She had kept her poo in her abdomen as a means of compensation.

My talks with Sylvie and her mother had provided some reference-points for those that took place with the little girl alone. Sylvie began to cut up the large fish that she had just drawn. She imagined that a mother could become pregnant by swallowing a penis-fish. On the same page, she got me to draw a small fish in the large fish's belly.

Then she told me her nightmare: 'A shower was running.' I was still none the wiser as to the content of her bad dream. I offered to make this a little clearer by drawing on the part of the paper that had escaped her scissors. Water was flowing from the head of the shower; a bear cub was lying in the water, probably having drowned. Sylvie then drew beside the water a mother transformed into a witch through her yellow hair and a mother wearing a crown.

During the school holidays, Sylvie had felt both jealous of the baby boy and envious of the mother who was capable of making a real baby and not just a large poo. Overwhelmed by the violence of her emotions, she had dreamt that her small rival was drowning in the urine with which she had flooded the mother's abdomen. She had not been able to tolerate her guilt feelings on waking up. She had regressed to the period in which she had split the mother's image into a horrible witch and a pretty young queen. I could only help Sylvie to put into words some 'action-representations' that her psychic scissors had cut into apparently meaningless fragments.

Understanding a dream brings about a sharing of emotion and imagination between the child and the adult. By telling his dream, the child is demonstrating his great trust in the adult. He is conveying to him that he is ready to share a deep psychological intimacy with him. In children's dreams, the content is often

also present in the form in which it is dreamt. Disturbed children confront us with primitive forms of dreaming. I shall now present one of these important times at which the child manages to adjust his mental organisation in order to establish its coherence by integrating a nightmare experience.

Sarah

Sarah had been coming to me for therapy sessions for five months.[7] Her difficulties at school were beginning to diminish and she was suffering from fewer psychic disturbances. I had gone on holiday and we had not seen each other for a month. On my return, I asked her if she had had any dreams. She replied by telling me the end of a dream. This was fairly indistinct: it was about a horrible witch. I offered to make it with some plasticine according to her instructions. I then went to look for the dolls. I took the witch that she knew well and I set about portraying the end of the dream.

The dream ended with the witch arriving; she took the baby and pushed it through the bowl of the loo. Sarah began to stick pencils representing wires into the plasticine witch's head. She then remembered how the dream began. I needed to help her put it into sentences. Here is our final account: 'The witch came into the bedroom. I was sleeping. She saw me first and she started attacking me (the elder sister sleeps in the same room as her). I woke up (in the dream). I saw that she had wires on her head like hair. She put me into a plastic bag. I was suffocating. I felt the wires that were hurting me. She took me to the loo. She put me in the bowl and pulled the flush. I choked.'

I knew that with Sarah it would be better to use the dream to find out the experience that had generated the latent thoughts than to try to interpret it. It was not appropriate just then to try to interpret the manifest content in order to discover the latent content. *The account reflected the psychic endeavour made by each of us to symbolise emotions that were difficult to articulate.* The little girl had avenged herself on her mother-therapist by subjecting it to what she had felt during this month in which she had been abandoned. She had inserted wires into the witch's head. She was making it feel the pain of the primitive thoughts that had assailed her while she was left alone, and perhaps also the suffering caused by my attempts to make her aware of the struggle that was taking place inside her.

Sarah had felt uneasy because she had retrieved memories in the form of strong emotions and violent feelings. She had spent two periods in hospital in the paediatric department at the ages of four months and one year, on each occasion for gastro-enteritis. The unconscious memory of this suffering had given rise to the first version of the dream: the baby has a horrible experience with a witch who comes to drown her in her vomit and excrement. The witch-mother is not capable of maternal reverie: she puts wire thoughts into the child's head instead of soothing thoughts. Sarah's memory of this distress was buried deep inside her. She had made me relive it through her transference when she had felt that I was capable of receiving and modifying it.

I concluded that the dream had initially reflected the ego under attack from psychotic anxieties, hence her being awoken by night terrors. However, Sarah now had a neurotic part that was capable of making compromises. This had enabled her to continue sleeping while dreaming that she had woken up. Her capacity for regression was now helping her to achieve a better integration of the different facets of her personality rather than entering a disorganised mental state.

8
Post-traumatic Dreams

'Black milk of daybreak we drink it at sundown
we drink it at noon in the morning we drink it at night'
Paul Celan.[1]

I have a sense that with this 'black milk of daybreak', Celan is providing a flash of insight into the repercussive qualities of the post-traumatic nightmare. Some severe mental disorders had made the poet highly sensitive to this blackness, leading him to write this *Death Fugue*.

Freud made constant reference to trauma throughout his work from the invention of psychoanalysis until his death. He adopted the term 'traumatic neurosis', which had been coined by a psychiatrist at the end of the 19th century. By borrowing this term, he acknowledged that a real event can have a profound and enduring destabilising impact on the psyche.

However, Freud left some fundamental questions unanswered. Can disorders with a traumatic origin exist independently of a preceding childhood conflict? Does the compulsion to repeat the terrifying situation in nightmares stem from neurotic difficulties that long pre-date the event?

The Second World War provided a far broader field of investigation than the First World War into the effects of psychic traumas. Unlike the previous war, this one did not spare the civilian populations. Moreover, it was the war in which extermination camps were instituted. Large numbers of children were subjected to aerial bombardments and mass evacuations. They also witnessed injuries, torture and the death of loved ones. They were separated from their parents in order to be protected from the combat, rationing and atrocities.

The importance accorded to psychic trauma in mental disturbances has constantly increased since the war. A simple and specific theory has superseded the complex conception of trauma in psychoanalysis. This led in the 1980s to the international recognition of 'post-traumatic stress syndrome' in children.[2] This syndrome is characterised by the re-emergence of the trauma in the form of repetitive games and nightmares. It was asked whether post-traumatic dreams were true nightmares. Some even argued that the model of the dream in childhood is not hallucinatory wish-fulfilment but post-traumatic oneiric activity.

There are currently two theories of traumatic pathology: on the one hand, traumatic neurosis and, on the other, post-traumatic stress syndrome. In very simple terms, I would suggest that with regard to stress, it is accepted that its intensity and suddenness provide an adequate explanation of the nature of the illness. However, with traumatic neurosis we take account of the impact of the trauma but we consider it in relation to the subject's level of tolerance and view the traumatic experience in the context of the individual's whole life.

POST-TRAUMATIC DREAMS CANNOT BE EXPLAINED
IN TERMS OF THE PLEASURE PRINCIPLE

A major turning-point occurred in Freud's work in the 1920s. The reasons for this change have been sought in biographies but the main factor seems to have been the impact of the carnage of the First World War. Following this, Freud placed the death drive beyond the pleasure principle. This hypothesis has remained highly controversial. The more human beings have demonstrated their capacity for destruction and self-destruction, the more steadfastly they have gazed in the opposite direction. In our time, the adjective 'schizophrenic' is now being used in a broad sense, as if in some implicit wish to deny that psychic conflict is an integral human characteristic.

Freud had discovered phenomena involving repetition across a very broad range of domains. It was difficult to explain these phenomena solely in terms of the striving for pleasure or an attempt to overcome unpleasurable experiences. He saw in them the mark of the 'daemonic', which is rather reminiscent of the demon that came to torment the dreamer in the nightmare. The study of dreams remained the most reliable method of exploring the deep psyche. People suffering from traumatic neurosis have dreams in which they find themselves back in the traumatic situation and wake up every time in terror. The trauma does not only disrupt the libidinal economy; it can also pose a threat to the subject's psychic integrity.

Freud provided an interesting scientific myth by reassessing the nature of traumatic neurosis. In very simple terms, he envisaged the original form of the living organism as an 'undifferentiated vesicle of a substance that is susceptible to stimulation'.[3] This lump of protoplasm would not have been able to survive if it had not had some means of protecting itself against strong excitations. An adaptive reaction led to the formation of a protective layer.

The outermost surface was thus transformed into a sort of membrane for absorbing excitations and allowing only a part of the excitation received from the external world to penetrate beyond it. This metaphor explains how the human being adapts to psychic trauma. If the organism wants to survive, it has to institute an internal apparatus, a mechanism for protecting it from excessively strong stimuli that originate from the external world. The baby normally develops the function of a protective shield. Based on this metaphor, psychic trauma is defined as something that can cause an extensive breach in the envelope that protects from excitations.

Freud established a tautological relationship between the protective shield apparatus and the psychic trauma. *This may result in the attribution of a traumatic origin to all psychic disturbances, just like the connection established between stress and trauma.* The following example seems to me to illustrate this problematic.

Brice

Recalling an event can sometimes instigate outside the sessions a dream work that has been lacking. I hope to provide an insight into this with the following example. Brice was nine years old at the time of our first meeting. Towards the end of the session, he remembered having had some nightmares in the past: 'Some dinosaurs were going to eat Mummy ... My friends were dead.' I had privately connected this with his father's absence since his birth.

Brice finally told me about a recent event that had distressed him. 'A month ago, I went to a place where there was a wasps' nest. I was stung seven times ... no, ten times. I touched it without realising. I was taken to see a doctor. He gave me a cortisone injection.' We continued to meet once a month, but we never talked about the incident again.

A year and a half later, Brice suggested drawing another picture together. I asked him about his dreams. He had just had a dream and he began to draw it while remaining silent. Finally, he talked to me about what he had drawn: 'A forest with lovely trees. There was a hole in a tree trunk. Suddenly, some wasps came out and attacked me. They stung me all over. I was walking there ... Afterwards, my mother took me to hospital (in fact, to a doctor's surgery). A wasp was still stuck on my wound. Mum told me: "I warned you not to go walking in the woods ..." The doctor was waiting for us outside. He took a stretcher and he put me on it. I was black all over because of the stings ... Mum was waiting outside with the car. When I came out, she asked me: "Are you all right?"' I thought again about his mother, who often came to fetch him when he left the consultation centre without even getting out of her car. I remembered the event that had actually occurred. Brice also remembered it. We managed to begin a dream work based on what had happened to him both in reality and in the dream.

CAN DREAMS RESOLVE TRAUMAS?

Some psychoanalysts have suggested that dreams can attenuate the shocks of the previous day and play an almost therapeutic role. Ferenczi also accorded great importance to the 'original traumatic factor' in the aetiology of neuroses at the end of his life when he was treating his patients using 'neocatharsis'. The retrieval of deeply buried memories convinced him that psychic trauma more generally results from inadequate or cruel treatment than from a constitutional hypersensitivity in the child. Ferenczi later revised the theory of dreams by attributing to them a 'traumatolytic function'.[4]

Sleep fosters not only wish-fulfilment but the return of raw post-traumatic impressions. A form of resolution can be achieved if the patient is encouraged to repeat and relive the event from beginning to end. Psychic trauma does not only occur in intense, dramatic and unexpected events. A set of events in daily life can have a traumatic impact if one person behaves violently towards another, if an apparently trivial incident has a destabilising effect, as we will see in the example that follows.

Cola

Cola looked physically older than her twelve years when she first came to see me with her parents. She had been born in Africa. When her mother emigrated to France, she had left Cola in her native country in the care of her grandparents, uncles and aunts. Her mother had married a Frenchman five years before the consultation took place. Cola had come over to live with them the following year. Her mother's husband had adopted her. However, this had done nothing to alleviate the bitterness she had felt since the couple had recently given birth to a boy. Every time this father took care of his son, Cola felt the pain of abandonment welling up inside her: her biological father had disappeared for ever without even having set eyes on her.

Cola had just received a warning at school because of her behavioural difficulties. Her violent outbursts were partly due to her difficulty in reaching the same level as pupils who had been educated entirely in France. The new father had tried to help her with her homework but he was feeling at the end of his tether. Cola had grown very fast in the last few months. She had developed post-exercise asthma (like her maternal grandmother). This had isolated her yet further from the other pupils. Her mother felt that Cola was shy and found group activities difficult to tolerate. Finally, the mother had told me that her daughter had been mistreated by her extended family, particularly by the mother's elder brother.

When she was alone with me, Cola told me that she had had nightmares when she first came to France. 'My grandmother is diabetic. I dreamt that the elder brother was hitting her.' In reality, it was Cola whom he had been beating. Cola called her eldest uncle 'great-uncle' because of some confusion between the generations. The next time, Cola was much better. She was no longer depressive. She talked to me again about the uncle who had mistreated her and who seemed to be suffering from a mental illness.

Cola told me a dream that seem to reflect the traumatic event: 'We were eating. I didn't know what I had done to him. He led me by the arm. He took me to his bedroom. He picked up a stick and he beat me. My other uncle (who was much younger) wanted to protect me but he beat him as well. (Do you remember what you had done?) You have to hold the plate between two fingers while you are eating. I had forgotten to do that. I still have a scar on my stomach.'

SEVERE TRAUMAS CAUSE NIGHTMARES

A historical review of studies on children generally begins with the work of Anna Freud and Dorothy Burlingham.[5] They observed some children who had been separated from their parents and placed in institutions during the Second World War. The main theoretical objective was to test the hypothesis put forward by Sigmund Freud in 1920. Could the repetitive games and nightmares be explained by a mode of functioning that preceded the onset of the pleasure principle and hallucinatory wish-fulfilment?

In 1945, an American psychiatrist drew a parallel between children's experiences in the operating theatre and soldiers' experiences on the battlefield.[6] The parallel between the battlefield and the other 'sphere of operations' is less surprising if we go back more than sixty years. Anaesthesia at that time was highly unsatisfactory, not to say dangerous. The child would be separated from his parents and his pain was often ignored. These aggravating factors have fortunately disappeared. The fact remains that the child undergoes a psychic trauma when he has an operation for a serious illness or a major accident. In France, Rufo emphasised in 1980 'the need for early intervention by child psychiatrists on-site in the hospital concerned'.[7] He regarded the dream as a superior means of understanding the anxieties that the child denies during the daytime.

Many studies were devoted in the 1950s and 1960s to children who were victims of collective disasters (for example, a tornado in the United States). The following decade, some paediatricians (re-)discovered physical maltreatment among children in hospital. Studies were also published about children living in conditions of endemic warfare (for example in Northern Ireland). The majority of studies on traumatogenic events concerned children who were living with their parents. The question was put as to whether the child's distress reflected the parents' own distress or if it was specific to him.

A series of American publications in the 1970s sought to provide an answer to this question. A second milestone was thereby reached following the initial war-time landmark. These publications became major reference-points because they related to a fairly large number of children who had been traumatised in the same way and had been studied over several years by the same team.

In 1976, over twenty pupils from a small town in California were abducted and buried alive, where they remained for more than twenty-four hours.[8] Terr examined almost all the children in the year they were abducted and she saw them again four to five years later. She established a 'control group' of non-traumatised children.

As with adults, the commonest type of dream consisted in the faithful reproduction of what had happened to them. However, the traumatised children also had night terrors that they did not remember on waking. The night terrors occurred more frequently among the children who were least able to express themselves in words. Post-traumatic nightmares and night terrors sometimes took place during the same night.

Over the course of time, elements from ordinary life were added to the repetition of the scenario of the catastrophe. For instance, a father or a mother, or brother or sister, might also be abducted and form part of the group of those buried alive. Some dreams were ultimately so disguised that the original event became difficult to recognise through a complex symbolism.

The traumatised children, like those in the control group, were able to dream about their own death. According to Terr, the children allowed themselves to dream about dying after the trauma because they no longer believed in their own invulnerability.[9] This suggested that it was the idea associated with the state of distress and not the actual experience that enabled the subject to begin to dream about his own death. Accordingly, the ego had been damaged because there were cognitive disturbances, such as the formation of false memories, faulty visual perceptions, temporal distortions and evasive thinking.

Terr argued against the received notion that the child's psyche proves to be more flexible than the adult psyche when confronted with a psychic trauma. The brief treatment instituted a few months after the trauma did not prevent a continuation of the symptoms until four years later. Although the most dramatic manifestations had disappeared, the impact of the trauma was still observable in daily life, in development of the personality and the attitude towards the future. It was nevertheless necessary to make some distinctions concerning this impact. The children who came from isolated or disturbed families presented more severe disturbances than the others. Similarly, the most vulnerable and most fragile children were more deeply affected by the trauma.

The tendency to consider the traumatic event as the prime if not sole source of childhood suffering was further reinforced in the 1980s for two reasons. On the one hand, children's testimonies began to be taken into consideration within the legal system. This required an understanding of how a traumatic event can have an enduring disturbing impact on a child and how he constructs the account of what has happened to him. On the other hand, the understanding of both stress and trauma led to a major water-shed in international classifications. In 1987, the American classification of mental disorders accorded a specific place to post-traumatic stress syndrome in children.

DREAMS PROVIDE A CONTEXT FOR EMOTION IN THE FORM OF EXPLANATORY METAPHORS

Hartmann devoted over twenty-five years to studying dreams in laboratories and in psychotherapy. He finally put forward a theory of dreams based on the consequences of psychic trauma.[10] Accordingly, the simplest form of dream is not that of a child who is enacting a hallucinatory wish-fulfilment but the post-traumatic dream. This choice is a somewhat problematic one, since civilised humankind has always sought to protect itself from unexpected and trying events.

Hartmann thought he had discovered a single process at work in all dreams. Dreaming enables broader and more intense connections to be made than in waking life. These connections are not random; they are dictated by the dreamer's dominant emotion. The dream provides a context for this emotion. When a dream is well organised, it appears more like a shifting metaphor than a cartoon strip. Hartmann considered the dream as an explanatory metaphor to the extent that it represents through analogies a part of what is happening in the dreamer's mind.

In the weeks or months following the trauma, dreaming seems to follow a general pattern. At the beginning, the trauma is intensely relived. However, dreams do not always reproduce the traumatic event in exactly the same form. An important change is often observed: the dream may contain an event that has not happened in reality.

The subject matter of the trauma very soon begins to combine in the dream with other material that has similar emotional tonalities. The person may develop an interest, for example, in other situations in which he has felt helpless, terrified or guilty. In some cases, this reactive linkage of earlier traumas brings people who are indirectly associated with the trauma back to the foreground. This linkage process extends further and further, such that the trauma plays an increasingly minor role in dreams. These finally revert to the form they took before the trauma.

In Hartmann's view, there are many parallels between dreaming and the psychotherapeutic process following a trauma. The main characteristic is that both provide a 'safe haven' in which an elaboration can be accomplished. In a therapy, this safe haven is more than a physical space because it involves the existence of secure boundaries and establishing a relationship of trust between patient and therapist. During the dreaming, especially in paradoxical sleep, the safe haven originates from a muscular inhibition that prevents action, or the acting out of the dream. Once the safe haven is established, the therapist allows the traumatised person to go back, to make connections between the trauma and the rest of his life and to talk about his life in various ways.

Hartmann attributed a quasi-therapeutic function to post-traumatic dreaming. The process consists in connecting the trauma with everything that is available in the memory and the imagination, based on the dreamer's dominant emotions. The scenes in post-traumatic dreams do not issue solely from sensory impressions recorded during the dramatic event. They are animated primarily by the prevailing emotions at that time. This model only applies in cases where the person manages to overcome his psychic trauma fairly well. He then emerges from it without developing a chronic form of post-traumatic stress syndrome. If the syndrome becomes chronic, the patient remains stuck in the repetition of his nightmares.

Although the quasi-therapeutic function emerges clearly after a trauma, it also exists in less overt forms in other dreams. Hartmann explained the substantial differences between human beings in terms of the capacity for dreaming and the style of dreaming. His study of nightmares had led him to make a distinction between individuals with thick psychic boundaries and those with thin boundaries. This contrast relates to an aspect of the personality that strives either to compartmentalise and to separate psychic material or to allow it to move around and to combine. Accordingly, the individual with thin boundaries is more open to inner experience and dreaming characterises a mental state with thin boundaries.

Part Three
Dreamy Child, Creative Child:
Dreams and Culture

9
The Formulation of Dreams and the Dreamer's Mentalisation

Freud established a distinction that he never rescinded between the dream as it exists in the dreamer's memory, which he called the 'latent content', and the material produced by the dream analysis, which he termed the 'manifest content'. It is the dream work that transforms the latent content into manifest content. The discovery of the latent content through the interpretation of the manifest content is a matter of technique. Freud always condemned those who seek the essence of the dream in its latent content. However, interest in the manifest content has been revived by the analysis of psychotics, psychosomatic and borderline cases and, particularly, of children. The manifest content can no longer be considered as a disguise or a distortion of unconscious material that occurs through censorship. The form taken by the dream reflects the dreamer's capacity for mentalisation.

IT IS ESSENTIAL TO FIND A WAY OF PUTTING THE EXPERIENCE OF THE DREAM INTO WORDS; THE INTERPRETATION OFTEN FORMS A SUPPLEMENT

It is often supposed that an adult's dream during an analysis is intended for interpretation. *Interpretation constitutes only one aspect of the therapeutic work. The formulation is always the starting-point and in the case of a child's dream it is often the end-point. When he manages to communicate the experience of the dream in words, the child has already gone a major part of the way.*

The patient has to discover the memory of an event that has been experienced mainly in the form of images and then transform it into a narrative. Because the dream relates only to internal reality and the internalisation of external reality, everything depends on a work of mental construction or reconstruction. The child is often unable to start to form a narrative without help from an adult.

If the patient has a good level of mentalisation, the analyst only needs to provide help in discovering what appears to have been forgotten, to enable something that was set aside to return and to allow that which has been rejected to emerge. If the patient has a low level of mentalisation, the analyst is called upon to a greater extent. He then has to work in collaboration with the patient or even provide a temporary psychic substitute.

A successful formulation is achieved through an overview of a manifest content with a newer and brighter façade. The analyst favours shaping material rather than dissecting it with a view to an immediate interpretation. This is achieved by linking memories, impressions, associations and comments. It concludes in a narrative of the dream experience that can be imparted and that could be published.

David

We are going to set these complex reflections alongside the popular knowledge of one of these children for whom dreaming is more of a worrying and disturbing experience than one conducive to integration. David met me for the first time when he was ten years old. He was accompanied by his mother, who was as reluctant as he was to know what they were seeking. We finally reached a compromise position: the child needed speech therapy for some difficulties at school.

In reality, David was suffering from many anxieties. If he had been an adult, I would have wondered if he was not bordering on delusional. David believed in ghosts. He was afraid that one might come and take him away. I discovered that he was having grandiose dreams, perhaps to compensate for his sense of helplessness in waking life. He would dream about the adventures of television heroes: he turned into Superman carrying a building in his hand.

David had begun speech therapy while I continued to see him from time to time. He liked watching horror films. He was expecting to see ghosts arrive at his house. He showed some reticence when talking about this. It was some information from his mother that enabled me to bring David to reveal his inner world.

One year after the therapy sessions had begun, David provided a dream narrative. He said he dreamt this every year: 'I am in bed. The door is opening. There are lots of little balls, the colour of wood. (David explained by pointing at the top of my desk.) They are coming towards me. A large ball of the same colour also comes towards me. It is going to explode on me. (How big is it?) Twice as big as the room … I lie down on the blanket. The ball touches me. (David gestured to indicate light contact.) It explodes. As if I were an electric shock.'

I could not establish any connection with what had happened either before or afterwards. Before, David had drawn a flower, then a road with a jagged line and finally a tree. Afterwards, he played with some Lego. I had asked him to help me to follow him and to understand. He only replied: 'It is imaginary.' (It is not worth talking about or it would be too dangerous to talk about.) David had learnt to fool people around him, usually by saying nothing and smiling. He was convinced that he would be thought mad if he talked about his irrational fears.

One day, David nevertheless explained to me what ghosts were: returning souls that can be seen reflected in mirrors. He began to draw in an automatic way. The outline of an old castle emerged, with a strange animal and some bizarre zigzags. David explained to me in a confused way that it was a form of energy that appeared in jolts. David managed to talk to me about his drawing as if it were a dream. 'There is a house like a castle. The (animal's) fur catches fire. Some muscles contract and that creates some jolts.' David agreed to explain to me what a dream was: 'A part of the brain (pointing to the back of his head) is like a cupboard in which memories are put away. The brain works on them.

It works harder at night. If a boy wants a pretty girl, he thinks about this all day: the girl comes back at night.'

THE CHILD DREAMS IN TERMS
OF HOW HE REPRESENTS THE WORLD

In the 1920s, Piaget studied how children represent the world in their dreams. He put four questions to some children: where do dreams come from? What do we dream with? Where are dreams? Why do we dream? Based on the answers he obtained to these questions, Piaget identified three approximately sequential stages.[1]

The *first stage* occurs in children aged five to six years old. These children think that dreams come from outside and remain external. The child situates the dream in the bedroom or the place in which it happens. The dream is an image or a voice that comes from outside to appear before his eyes. This image is not real, in that it does not represent real elements. But it nevertheless exists in an objective way. When we ask the child if someone next to him would be able to see the dream, he answers yes. However, the parents and the social environment then undeceive the child to a greater or lesser degree. Finally, the dream is not just like any other phenomenon but is an emotionally charged event. This explains why children almost always attribute the images in their dreams to people rather than to things.

These stages should not be understood in a rigid way but as indications of a general trend. Personality type and intellectual level can also influence the representation of the dream, as the following example will show.

Nicolas

Nicolas was coming up to five years old when his mother decided to consult me about his violent behaviour. He had difficulty controlling his behaviour. When he encountered an obstacle (material or human), he became violent and he ran amok. He seemed to have an anger inside him that was always ready to erupt. From the time he started at nursery school, Nicolas had become violent towards other children. He struck me as a strange boy, rather intelligent but extremely troubled by his inner world.

Nicolas had many nightmares that he found difficult to talk about. It may have been because of these that he was still peeing in bed. I had only been able to make out: 'I am afraid a monster (or a ghost) will come and take me away.' Nicolas told me that he would hit nice children when they changed, putting on a nasty voice. He gave me the impression that he was functioning at the boundary of psychosis.

We continued to meet for therapy sessions. Nicolas preferred using plasticine to drawing. Every time, he wanted me to make him some monsters. He would immediately attack them with his fists or pierce them with the modelling stick. I would insist every time that he talk to me about his nightmares. I told him that I could not make interesting or funny monsters without having some idea about what he was seeing at night.

I found one of the early narratives incomprehensible. 'The monster was coming to tickle me. (Under your feet?) He was twisting my toes.' Nicolas very soon got into the habit of making me repeat the same series of actions. I would make a monster and he would attack it sadistically and literally tear it to pieces. I became the bad one because I was making the monsters. Nicolas then brought some small animal figures (Pokemon or Digimon figures). He used them to attack and destroy my monsters.

One day, he managed to describe to me a nocturnal vision, a dream that had come from outside and stayed outside him. 'A monster with forty eyes, slimy with flowing blood. (How big was it?) Like Daddy. (What did it do to you?) It was torturing my feet. (How did this end?) I put the light on. It went away because it was afraid of the light.' I made some monsters that he massacred with shouts of joy (so loud that his mother could hear them in the waiting room). He would be particularly triumphant if he could snatch an appendage: a nose, a head or hat, or a willy.

Another day, Nicolas also enjoyed using the intermediary of his plastic animals not only to attack but also to eat my plasticine monsters. He told me about a nightmare that he could remember only vaguely. 'I went through a door. There was a very nasty man. He looked like an extra-terrestrial. He wanted to catch me and kill me with an axe.' I asked him where the monsters came from. 'From planet Zorg. (Could they have come from your head? Nicolas was surprised by my question. He paused to think before replying.) Yes, they come from the head-planet.' I realised that the first stage was coming to a close and that Nicolas was beginning to represent the world differently in his dreams.

THE DREAM GRADUALLY BECOMES A FORM OF THOUGHT

The *second stage* corresponds to the seven- to eight-year-old child. The dream comes from inside him but it remains external. The child has discovered or learnt that the dream comes from his head, from his thoughts. He locates the image in the bedroom, beside him since he can look at it. The child gradually manages to distinguish the image from the thing that is represented. If the child draws what he has dreamt, he situates the dream beside the bed, in front of the dreamer who is looking at it. The discovery that the dream stems from thought gradually alters how it is situated in space, hence the evocative formula: 'Can one see thought? *Yes, in dreaming.*'[2]

The *third stage* occurs in the nine- to ten-year-old child. 'The dream is internal and of internal origin.'[3] The child first considers the dream as an external picture produced by things and then by the head. When the child begins to locate the dream inside him, he represents it as a picture, a story in the form of images that are imprinted inside the eye. They begin to use expressions such as 'You think that', 'It seems as if', 'It's as if'. The dream does not become an internal and imaginal form of thought until around the age of eleven: '[The dream is] *something you think when you are asleep.*'[4]

Farid

We are going to see how a child moved from the first to the second stage during a course of psychotherapy. Farid was just five years old when I first saw him with his mother. She had waited till the middle of the summer holidays to decide on this, although the school had advised her to have a consultation at the beginning of the school year. She would only admit that he was dreamy. I had had to undertake an anamnesis to discover that he had changed a great deal after the birth of his sister. She had been born a year and a half after him. He had lost his good appetite, and been awoken by night terrors. His rather chaotic psychic organisation made it difficult for him to confront an omnipresent anxiety, although he was carrying out checks and rituals. A raw and direct fantasmatic expression, dominated by aggression, had indicated to me a pre-psychotic personality.

At our first meeting, Farid began by playing with some plasticine. He piled up balls in a rudimentary way to build a mountain. I found it difficult to understand what he was saying to me. He talked very fast, externalising everything that was going on in his mind. He almost plunged me into total confusion. Suddenly, he wanted to go and wash his hands. He took some time to evacuate his faeces in the loos.

When he came back to my office, he wanted to draw. He started by drawing a strange man with a rectangular body and a circular head. He scrawled red over the body. 'It's bleeding. (Why?) He has been stabbed with a knife.' Farid then drew an identical man to the first, who was stabbing with a knife. He drew a line around both the men. It seemed to me that the man was holding a syringe rather than a knife. I concluded that Farid was telling me how dangerous he felt his attraction towards me to be.

I shall move straight on to a drawing that he produced after two years of therapy. One time, Farid wanted to draw my portrait. I watched him drawing in silence. It seemed to me that this must be an image from a dream. He agreed with this. He still tended to confuse meeting me in my office with finding me at night in his home. His blurred mental boundaries and his sense of omnipotence meant that he could accord the same force of reality to both types of event. I noticed that Farid's mentalisation had distinctly improved when he produced a drawing in which he was lying on a bed, sleeping, next to an enormous image of my head.

We talked a little about each of our representations here. This gave Farid the idea of connecting us symbolically through the dream. He drew an enormous bubble around my head with a dotted line, as in a cartoon. Looking from one side to the other revealed at one moment my thought containing Farid sleeping and, at the next, Farid dreaming about me. In any case, he had unconsciously found the relationship that connects the patient lying on the couch with his analyst.

If we go back to the first drawing, we can see the path that has been taken. Farid had transformed the initial situation in which a man's stomach was being pierced by the syringe of another man. We were no longer enclosed in a shared

membrane; we could converse through our respective mental bubbles. It is true that I was still a vast, disturbing, voracious figure. However, he also knew that I was able to receive and tolerate everything that came from him. I had survived his destructive attacks and he had been able to identify in part with my capacity to dream about the content of our relationship.

MENTALISATION INFLUENCES HOW WE DREAM

I have used the term 'mentalisation' here because it has a broad range of possible meanings. 'Mentalisation' is a general term that can be applied to the processes of representation, symbolisation and abstraction.[5] Freud emphasised the need to master a part of the drive energy through psychic work. This work of binding restricts the free circulation of excitations while also creating interconnected mental representations.

In France, the concept of mentalisation was introduced in the 1960s by psychoanalysts treating psychosomatic disorders. It refers to an activity that is undertaken very early to transform somatic excitations into symbolised mental content and to maintain this symbolic form. Mentalisation occurs on a spectrum, on which the psychic quality is absent at one end and fully present at the other. Mentalisation is a complex task that consists in producing psychic material. In general terms, its purpose is to generate a 'preconscious'. This is constituted by psychic material that is neither immediately accessible to consciousness nor part of the unconscious.

According to Marty, the characteristics of the preconscious can be assessed using three criteria:

- thickness: the greater the number of layers, the smaller the possibility of a disorganisation caused by unimaginable traumas;
- fluidity of connections, which should ensure free play of associations;
- constancy: mental representations must function in a permanent and stable way.[6]

In my view, the capacity for dreaming is closely connected with the degree of mentalisation. This can be categorised according to several levels. At the lowest level, the individual has only superficial, unstable and limited mental representations that are devoid of affective and symbolic cathexes. At the highest level, the individual is suffering from the neuroses described in psychoanalysis. He has rich, stable and deep mental representations that are strongly cathected with symbolism and affect. Here we can recognise Freud's mental functioning during his self-analysis, which served as a model for the theory of dreams. The repression that operates in the classical neuroses presupposes a high level of mentalisation. Only material that has already been mentalised through an intersubjective matrix is subject to repression.

THE REFLECTIVE FUNCTION EMERGES
IN THE MOTHER–CHILD INTERACTION

Fonagy has also discussed mentalisation. However, his theory is based on the analysis of narcissistic or borderline patients.[7] He thus distinguished two complementary objectives in psychoanalysis. With borderline patients, it is necessary first to assess their disconcerting and chaotic mental functioning and, most particularly, their capacity for mentalisation. However, with classical neurotic patients, it can be enough to lift the repression that is inhibiting or disrupting fairly well developed mental functioning.

Many analytic patients have to be helped to dissolve inhibitions and overcome blocks in mentalisation before conflicts as such can be addressed. As a result of the absence or weakness of their capacity for mentalisation, borderline patients have too strong a tendency to act out the transference. They are not sufficiently capable of using their mental representations.

Fonagy's starting-point was in the theory of mind that emerged at the end of the 1970s. This theory gained a certain renown when it put forward a new conception of autism. It swept aside the psychoanalytic theories, particularly Bettelheim's metaphor of the empty fortress.[8] The hypothesis was that autism originates from a deep disturbance in cognitive development: the autistic child is incapable of developing a coherent world view, a representation of his own thoughts and desires or, consequently, those of others.[9]

It is difficult to summarise a theory that borders on philosophy. In concise terms: at around the age of three years, children begin to attribute beliefs, desires and psychic states to other people. The attribution of psychic states to other people confers meaning on human behaviour and enables it to be predicted. It seems likely that this aptitude in relation to others is associated with the child's capacity to identify his own experiences and to attribute a significance to them.

The capacity to ascribe beliefs to others inaugurates a 'second order' in mental representation. This is an important stage in the developmental path that leads from a relative egocentrism to socialisation. From birth to the age of five months, the infant develops through affective signals that are exchanged facially between his mother and himself. At this stage, interactions are only mentalised in an egocentric way because the child does not need to form a representation of his caregiver's thoughts and feelings.

Mental representations become organised from six to eighteen months of age. During this period, the child gradually acquires the capacity to adjust his own mental state to the mother's or another person's mental state. Fonagy has proposed the term 'reflective function' for the predisposition to understand one's own and other people's behaviour.[10] He carefully distinguished the reflective function from self-reflection or introspection. This latter refers to the explicit knowledge of psychic states that is obtained from introspection. The reflective function is defined by the capacity to confer explicitly and automatically a meaning on behaviour and therefore to regulate it actively. It has an enormous impact on the form and organisation given to the self.

Most mothers are capable of understanding their child's mental states. They facilitate the child's understanding of other people by interacting with him. On the other hand, anxious or depressed mothers are at risk of hindering the operation of the reflective function. If the mother–child interactions are characterised by a persistent lack of reciprocity, the child can become vulnerable, in the sense that he will be more likely to react to a subsequent trauma through a dissociation.

Studies of child development have often only considered daytime events. However, dreaming is the cradle of thought. It is through dreaming that the child begins to operate the reflective function. If he manages to communicate the experience of the dream, he thereby differentiates himself better from other people and increases his capacity for abstraction.

10
Foetal Dreams

The high proportion of active or seismic sleep in the foetus has attracted much curiosity. A certain amount of oneiric activity has been thought to occur as early as gestation because this active sleep seems to be a precursor of paradoxical sleep. The more general question has been posed as to whether the foetus has a psychic life. A rudimentary mental life would thus develop in the uterus as part of the process through which active sleep modifies the sensory information received by the foetus. Accordingly, it is the encounter between two beings who are gradually becoming separate that leads to the transformation of the biological dream into a psychological dream.

As children grow up, they try to articulate the experience of the dream, which has a biological foundation, and its narrative formulation, which falls within the sphere of language. Children are capable of constructing autobiographical narratives from the age of around three or four years old. The emergence of this advanced capacity for self-expression through language marks a very important stage in the development of intersubjective relationships and social interaction. Children become able to relay the experiences they have had and impart them to other people.[1]

ADOLESCENT CRISIS OR PRIVATE MADNESS?

Before imagining what foetuses dream about, we are going to make the acquaintance of an adolescent girl whose imagination developed outstandingly during a mourning process that was proving very difficult. She also revealed a remarkable capacity for producing a narrative of her dream life in playful formulations. 'What is invisible begins in the eye. This contains the counterpart of external space – our inner space. The gaze acts as the ferryman between one and the other.'[2]

Claudine

Claudine had come to consult me with her mother when she was thirteen years old. It fairly soon became clear that she was coming because she was having difficulty mourning for her paternal grandparents. Her grandfather had died of a heart attack eight years earlier. Her grandmother had been buried only a year before the consultation after suffering from cancer for two years. Claudine would have been less sad if her mother had not been fonder of her parents-in-law than of her own parents. This mother had cared devotedly for the ill woman for many months.

It was in June that Claudine had lost her grandmother. She had been having difficulty both getting to sleep and staying asleep since November. She was constantly having very rich and astounding dreams that were difficult to grasp. The essential element was to find her parents every night, in order to share their life between heaven and hell or to travel to distant imaginary islands. In the therapy session, the mother had been able to take an active part in our conversation.

At the next session, Claudine was waiting for me alone. She had followed a suggestion made by her mother. She was holding a piece of card on which she had drawn the three worlds of her dreams. This seemed to be highly complex but very well structured. Closely in touch with her own generation, Claudine had had the idea of transposing her world of dreams into the context of a video game.

The first world looked like a large building with three storeys above ground level and three storeys underground. It was possible to move between the different levels using a lift. As would be expected, paradise was at the very top and hell was right at the bottom. Claudine had included a cafeteria, a cinema, recreational workshops and a shopping centre between the two.

The second world was populated with ghosts. The card was almost entirely covered with a crowd of human beings that Claudine knew or had known. Each ghost was constituted of an agglomeration of a hundred or so stars. Finally, the third world had only just been sketched because the islands were very far away. This was probably going to take on a more concrete form because Claudine and her elder sister were about to go on holiday with their maternal grandparents to a paradisiacal island in the Pacific.

The forthcoming holiday was giving rise to some separation anxiety both in the girls and in the mother. This all-consuming reverie had not prevented Claudine from leading a very full social life. She was dancing and playing a musical instrument. She was doing fairly well at school. She complained that she was being ill-treated by a pupil in her class. Finally, she was also trying to choose between two boys who were in love with her in her class.

Contrary to appearances, Claudine's mental balance lacked stability. We talked about her sister, who had been hospitalised for anorexia nervosa. Claudine had not been able to see her grandparents' faces in her dreams since the end of the previous year. Her universe had become complicated because the grandparents had become split into good and bad figures. The bad ones were stopping her from working efficiently at school.

This young adolescent's imaginary creation was reminiscent of the imaginative journey undertaken by Dante in the Middle Ages in Italy. The poet gave allegorical expression to a journey through the sites of the Christian after-life. Claudine, living in the 21st century, replaced hell, purgatory and paradise with three sections of a video game. However, her construction also resembled the ravings of an adult paraphrenic.

The description of the paraphrenias dates back to the beginning of the 20th century. Psychiatrists had been intrigued by the contrast between a delusional activity that was often fantastical in nature and the maintenance of fairly good contact with reality. There is still some logic within the delusional construction, although it often expands in a florid way. Imaginative delusions occur in the same register but they expand in a disordered and diffluent way and are devoid of logic. They border on mythomania. Claudine did not remotely resemble a mythomaniac. When she came back from her trip to a faraway island with her maternal grandparents, her obsession with her private theatre had almost completely ceased. It was beginning to fade, just like the image of her dead paternal grandparents. Claudine quickly abandoned it. Her invention testified to the rich imagination of the hysterical personality.

WHAT DO FOETUSES DREAM ABOUT?

Claudine may have begun to accord an important place in her life to dreams at a very early age. Is it too fanciful to speculate as to what she might have dreamt about in her mother's womb, from which she seemed to have great difficulty separating? 'Through metaphorical thought, it is possible to give the impression of understanding with images. Other methods will be required to find a cause.'[3] Cyrulnik created a metaphor for what the adult can imagine concerning the thoughts of the foetus. I share his view that active sleep brings about an integration of the diffuse sensoriality of the foetus. The foetus spends a large proportion of his time in a biological dream. He supplies his dream with sensory information perceived during his waking hours. 'This intra-uterine experience, sustained by sensoriality and interpreted biologically by rapid sleep (sleep with dreams) reveals the emergence of intra-uterine psychic life.'[4]

Ultrasound has shown that the pregnant woman's foetus experiences REM sleep. This can easily be detected during the mother's sleep because active sleep is accompanied by jolts and impulses in various sets of muscles. A connection has been observed between the onset of dreaming in the mother and seismic sleep in the foetus. It has been asked whether these are synchronised. It has also been argued that one can be triggered by the other.

At around the ninth month, the foetus takes more initiative in his behaviour instead of reacting to what comes from his mother. He displays an emerging autonomy by instigating a separation. This first arises in the rhythmicity that structures his perception of time. The representation that is established at the end of pregnancy is supplied by sensory information that has become familiar through the biological dream. The separation generated by the de-synchronisation of the foeto-maternal rhythms turns time into an object of perception; this leads the foetus to structure the sensoriality and to attribute meaning to the senses.

Accordingly, the prototype for the psychic apparatus forms in the encounter between mother and foetus, between the events that arouse maternal emotions and the way in which the foetal nervous system perceives and records the external manifestations of this maternal experience. Mental life before birth is thus constructed during encounters between a proto-mental apparatus: the sleep accompanied by dreams and the sensory and emotional experience provided by the mother. 'It is the encounter between two beings who are gradually becoming separate that provides mental life with its impetus.'[5]

Active sleep enables us to reprocess the sensory events that have been stored in a raw state in the memory. These sensations have strong pleasurable or unpleasurable connotations. The biological intermingling provides an impetus for the emergence of representation. A few days after birth, the baby already has a neuropsychic apparatus that is able to receive, filter and organise his experience and his memories of it. This then enables the baby to recognise in the external world a stable form that is capable of feeding, protecting and loving him. The maternal reverie later gives him the possibility of transforming his perceptions into material that can be thought and represented. Ultimately, the baby manages to instigate the psychological dream. There is still a long way to go before language enables him to impart the dream experience through autobiographical narratives.

FOETAL LIFE IS NOT SOLELY BIOLOGICAL

Do we enter the world as a *tabula rasa*, a slate that is empty of any inscriptions? This long-standing philosophical debate has always troubled the psychoanalytic community. It has erupted violently on the subject of psychological birth. Some argue that the infant does not come into the world with an apparatus for having thoughts and that he has no ego. By contrast, others take the view that biological birth itself instigates a mental life. The baby starts to feel emotions and to have proto-thoughts as soon as he encounters other human beings.

In 1973, an English analyst posed the question: 'Does prenatal mental life exist?'[6] He acknowledged modestly that he did not have a great deal to say on the matter but that it was an interesting question. He hypothesised the existence of pre-natal imprints. These had to be decipherable if symbols formed earlier than had been supposed. This would suggest first and foremost the existence of traumatic imprints left by threats to the foetus during pathological pregnancies.

Around fifteen years later, an Italian analyst stated not only that there was mental life before birth but also that there was a continuity between this and the mental life observed after birth. Piontelli had first conducted an analytic observation of babies.[7] She had had cause on several occasions to regret her lack of knowledge concerning the nine months of the gestation period. She decided to undertake some indirect observation of the foetus through ultrasound as a prelude to direct infant observation. Piontelli first observed some single pregnancies before going on to study twin pregnancies.

Since the 19th century, twins have been the subject of scientific studies seeking to determine the proportion of innate and acquired characteristics. Piontelli noticed that every twin very early manifested his own temperament. Similarly, every pair of twins also seemed very quickly to establish their mode of relating to each other. Both the temperament of each twin and the behaviour of the pair seemed to continue along the same lines after they were born. Finally, psychological birth can occur at different developmental stages. In some cases, it occurs well before biological birth and, in others, considerably later.

DREAMING PERPETUATES MAGICAL THINKING

In the early 1960s, Fraiberg wrote a short book summarising the current state of knowledge concerning early childhood in American psychoanalysis (combined with Piaget's psychology). She used an evocative title – *The Magic Years* – to refer to the first five years of life.[8] She stated that this period of childhood lies within us like a buried city. When we relive these years through children, we become strangers who have trouble finding their way. These are magic years because the child regards himself as a magician. He believes that his actions and thoughts can cause events.

They are also magic years because adults imagine that the child lives in an enchanted world in which his deepest aspirations can be fulfilled. As a psychoanalyst, Fraiberg knew that a magic world is a changing world haunted by ghosts. Before managing to construct reality, the child has to do battle with the threatening creatures that have emerged from his imagination, as well as the real dangers of the external world. Parenthood is often based solely on the adult's intuitive understanding of his child. The educational methods used by parents must take account of the child's developmental stage and his emotional and cognitive capacities.

Let us suppose that a child believes that a crocodile is hiding under his bed after encountering one in a nightmare. The two-year-old child's crocodile will not be the same as the five-year-old child's in psychological terms. The animal will almost certainly have grown up with the child. It will have become more complex than on the day it first took shape. Furthermore, we do not behave in the same way towards a two-year-old child and the same child at the age of five. The two-year-old child is just beginning to speak. He is convinced as he goes to bed that an animal is really there under his bed. The five-year-old can consider the problem with an adult. If his mentalisation is good enough, he will be able to have two kinds of thoughts as to what to believe about the crocodile.

In the early 1980s, early childhood was no longer conceived in terms of magic years in developmental psychology. Through direct observation and experimentation, everything was confidently explained without reference to 'magic'. Stern managed to construct a very detailed picture of the early years of life.[9] Accession to the world of language constitutes a crucial stage but the young child has the capacity, before language, to organise his experience in a proto-mental way. However, we should bear in mind that oneiric life, which is the prime focus of this book, was left to one side by both Fraiberg and Stern.

No one who finds themselves with a young child, watching and taking care of him, can help attributing needs, feelings or thoughts to him from one moment to the next. There is one obvious truism for those who remember their early childhood as a buried city: we were all babies at the outset. We have ways of guessing the inner life of the small child or inventing it for him. The need or the desire to know what is going on in the baby's head is familiar to every ordinary parent. The parent finds himself putting himself in his baby's shoes, entering into his thoughts and identifying with him.

The adult's response depends mainly on how he himself has been treated in childhood and how his own parents interpreted his behaviour. The baby needs the maternal reverie in order to be able to muse about his perceptions and emotions in turn. This maternal reverie is a means of interpreting what the baby is feeling and experiencing. It helps to familiarise him with his own experience. He does not know exactly what he is feeling, at which point he is feeling it, what he wants or what is tormenting him. The adult's empathy and understanding help him to pinpoint and then to define his emotions, feelings and wishes.

The parents compose a form of biography by memorising day after day the sensations and intentions they have attributed to their child. As he becomes the member of a family, the child is subjected to rules and customs that help or hinder him in constructing his own experience. The child does not mature in a linear way but in stages.

Stern suggests that the child has experienced five successive worlds by the time he is four years old. Each time the child takes an important step in maturation, he enters a 'new world'. However, he never completely abandons the previous one. The new world supplements the previous one rather than replacing it. The child, the adolescent and the adult experience several worlds that are superimposed on each other without ever completely eliminating those that went before. It is their interconnections that are the source of the rich variety in human experience.

Stern suggests that a social self emerges at a very early age through interpersonal relations. The stages, enriched with oneiric life, are as follows.

- At six weeks old, the child lives in the first of these worlds: the world of sensations. He is sensitive to raw experience. The maternal reverie is indispensable for transforming sensory and emotional materials into materials for dreams. Autistic and congenitally blind children may continue to cling to this world of sensations, which is not adapted either to dreams or to advanced thought.
- At four months old, the child enters a primary social world. He remains in close connection with his mother. Biological dreaming still predominates.
- At twelve months, the child discovers that he has a mind and that others also have minds. He becomes aware of the existence of wishes. The onset of psychological dreaming begins to be identifiable to observers.
- At twenty months, the child enters the world of language. He begins to impart his nocturnal experience.
- At four years old, the child is capable of speaking for himself. He can construct an autobiographical account that he can relate to an interlocutor. The child has the capacity to dream although the construction of reality is far from complete.

THE LONG JOURNEY TOWARDS
AUTOBIOGRAPHICAL NARRATIVES

The child can impart what he is experiencing to an adult well before he is able to make use of language. Interaction first manifests itself in the direct imitation of behaviour. By doing what the other person is doing, the baby begins to participate in a shared experience. Towards the end of the first year, he becomes aware that a feeling can arise in response to a similar feeling and that an experience can overlap with another person's experience. He discovers that he can impart not only his actions but also his emotional experience to other people.

The child begins to speak at around two years of age. Infant observation has led to a view of psychic reality that differs from Freud's theory. Accordingly, with the emergence of language the child has two psychic realities rather than one. His imagination leads him in a form of make-believe to create another psychic world in addition to that which represents everyday life. This 'second form of psychic reality' has adaptive properties. The child uses memorable aspects of his past to try out new possibilities in the present. In doing so, he orientates himself to some extent towards the future.[10]

Freud created the concept of psychic reality to indicate that subjective experience has a similar coherence and consistency to the world of objects. This subjective experience comprises thoughts, feelings and fantasies, but also representations based on perceptions of the external world. In the classical view, this subjective world is constructed without any concern as to whether it precisely reflects the world of experience or another person has a similar view of it. The intuition always belongs to a particular individual. The object of this intuition can only be recognised if each person can make it comprehensible to himself and to other people. It therefore has to be possible for psychic reality, as an individual's subjective experience, to be imparted and communicated.

A 'second form of psychic reality' can be contemplated to the extent that the child's imagination becomes directed towards the future. This occurs when the child develops a capacity for narration. This enables him to process the realist representation of the everyday world, as well as his imaginary productions in the make-believe world. Both can be communicated through the organisation of thought in narrative form. Narration introduces the possibility of coherently providing substitute worlds and imagining possible worlds alongside real worlds.[11]

The child can convey what he is experiencing to an adult long before he is able to use language. Interaction first manifests itself in the direct imitation of behaviour. The accession to the world of language opens up new communicative and imaginative horizons. The baby is compelled to modify everything that originated from gestural imitation. Language enables him to share what he has experienced. However, the most important change occurs at the age of three years, when the child becomes capable of constructing rudimentary narratives that involve temporal progression. He constructs his narrative with a culmination point, a central event towards which all the elements converge.

Language also enables him to construct the account of an event with an interlocutor. The adult serves as a support and a model for the child.[12] At the beginning, the adult provides a narrow framework for the child's words by asking him detailed questions about matters of daily routine. He introduces most of the contents of the narration. Ultimately, it is the child who provides the new information and also who selects it from beyond the daily routine. At the age of four, the child is capable of speaking for himself. He can outline an autobiographical narrative and tell it to an interlocutor.

Narration is not composed exclusively of information; it is also steeped in emotions. In fact, it modulates and regulates emotions. This begins in the facial interaction between the young child and the adult. Direct expression is adequate for obtaining more affection or emotional comfort. At a second stage, the child uses autobiographical narration to gain some distance from the experience he has undergone. Dreams provide a model as he becomes able to observe his psychic life and turn it into a narrative.

The commonest example is that of the two-year-old child at bed-time. Separation is often mentioned in the dialogue that precedes and accompanies going to bed. As long as the parent is present, he modulates the excessively strong emotions, the anxieties, both through his attitude and through his words. When the parent is no longer there, the child has to provide this regulation for himself with what he tells himself in his own head or by telling it to an imaginary interlocutor. Finally, when the child goes to sleep, regulation and elaboration take place through a form of visual thinking.

11
From the Mental Image to Visual Thinking

This brings us on to a consideration of the normal development of mental images. Piaget studied imaginal representation. The mental image does not simply reproduce a perception; it also plays a part in imagining what has not yet occurred. The mental image becomes a dream thought when it contains a symbolic dimension.

Psychoanalysis has established that a rich symbolic life exists long before speech, although symbolisation reaches its highest level in language. The capacity to dream depends on the operation of visual thinking.

THE MENTAL GAZE AND VISUAL THINKING

According to Freud, in many people thought progresses towards consciousness through visualisation. 'In some way, too, it [thinking in pictures] stands nearer to unconscious processes than does thinking in words, and it is unquestionably older than the latter both ontogenetically and phylogenetically.'[1] Later, Melanie Klein suggested that symbolism begins in the infant's earliest relationship with his mother.

Lewin went one step further by referring to the 'pictorial past'.[2] He argued that there is a period of childhood during which a set of meaningful experiences is recorded in the form of visual traces that determine the sensory quality of early memories and fantasies before fading, or even disappearing altogether. In any case, imaginal thought continues in dreams. In a dual process, images can be transformed into words and vice versa.

I also consider that there is a visual stage on the path that leads towards words and abstract thought. The child initiates a thought-activity by playing with the images that are preserved during the object's absence. The mother's face may act as a precursor to the psychic mirror. Her image endures when the object disappears. This is the onset of a thought activity. Its foundation in the gaze brings a specifically psychic dimension to the primordial experience of the mouth and skin.

What has been experienced in relation to the external world is reorganised and schematised through the imaginative possibilities of oneiric activity.[3] Before speech, the child thinks not in images but with images and schemas. He produces thought and dreams not only with mental images but also with intermediate representations between what he has perceived through his senses and his developing categories of understanding.[4]

At the same time, the representation of the separation between the baby and his mother, between internal reality and the external world, engenders a compromise formula that can be shared collectively: the formula of a transitional space, as the site of culture. The child integrates an increasing number of verbal signs as speech transforms his daytime experiences. He completes the transition from sensations and emotions to feelings and concepts. The communication of dreams often turns out to be very rich because oneiric experience is organised by visual thinking before it is formulated as a narrative.

CHILDREN'S MENTAL IMAGES

In studies of dreams, I have focused on those that accord a role to mental imagery in psychological life. Piaget first examined rational thought, which is brought into operation by the emerging logical and mathematical framework of reality. He then turned towards intuitive, representational or imaginal thought.[5] He decided to investigate its actual genesis instead of considering it as a stage that ultimately forms part of the set of abstract operations. Like play, symbolic thought and so on, imaginal representation continues to exist independently.

Piaget did not have a psychoanalytic objective. He was not interested in the creative imagination, only in the connections between imaginal representation and thought processes. He asked whether or not the image constituted the source of intellectual operations. In fact, Piaget was far from indifferent to the creative imagination as it manifests itself in dreams, for example. He traced a line of descent between the aspect of adult thought that remains individual, imaginal and partly incommunicable and the child's pre-operational thought (and, beyond this, the 'primitive mentality' discussed by Lévy-Bruhl).[6]

The mental image can be obtained only indirectly, through the description that the subject provides of his introspection, his drawing of it and the selection of one drawing from several models of gestural reproduction. An intermediate system is thereby demonstrated between the primary perception and its infinite variations and the concepts expressed in speech. This system is made of perceptual schemas.

Piaget established a fundamental distinction between:

- reproductive images, which develop from the pre-operational level (before seven to eight years of age from the onset of the semiotic function) and
- anticipatory images, which represent that which has yet to occur and only develop after the level of concrete operations.

Piaget was surprised to discover that the reconstitutions, re-anticipations and anticipations played a larger role than he had anticipated. Every mental image requires a reconstitution that contains a predictive aspect.

Like representational knowledge, no elementary thought could be formulated, rendered intrinsically intelligible to oneself and others without the production of signs and symbols. Language does not fulfil all the functions that can be anticipated from the semiotic process. There are a great many individual experiences that can only be conveyed poorly by language because it is too abstract. The individual gives concrete form to the meaning of the words he uses through mental images. If we want to evoke in thought what has been perceived, the system of verbal signs has to be duplicated by a system of imaginal symbols.

Mental imagery has given rise to philosophical debates and scientific investigations. The 'imagery debate' has produced two opposing sets of theories: either mental images are more or less exact reproductions of external reality or they are nothing but linguistic descriptions.[7]

The arrival of the digital camera and the scanner lend support to the thesis that mental images reproduce external reality based on the computer model. Accordingly, they resemble the images projected on the cathode-ray tube, when information from the computer is given material form.

Even if it had been produced on the basis of coded information, the mental image would function like a reproduction. It would be a 'quasi-reproduction'. It could be produced according to an identical principle to that which enables the image formed on the retina to be reproduced on the cerebral cortex. What matters is that each component of the image should correspond to a component or an aspect of the external object.

Conversely, other cognitivists consider that mental images are like linguistic complexes. This thesis seems to be further removed from the individual's everyday experience. It would be less plausible were it not for the fact that verbal thinking follows on from visual thinking and if we did not use words to discuss mental images. In any case, it is still accurate to state that images are sometimes quasi-reproductions and sometimes linguistic descriptions.

THE HIGHER-FUNCTIONING AUTIST THINKS IN IMAGES

The nature of a function is usually deduced from its associated difficulties. The higher-functioning autist is an interesting case in point here because despite suffering from a severe disturbance in social interaction, he is not handicapped by a delay in linguistic development or lack of intelligence. He is able to convey what is happening inside him. Grandin has also shown how she thinks in images. It seems to me that this visual thinking serves to compensate for the inadequacy of her dream thoughts.

Temple Grandin suffers from Asperger's syndrome (one of the higher-functioning forms of autism). Although the quality of her social interactions has been affected, she has been able to lead a social life that is close to normal. She has written a book that, among others, has given valuable insight into the processes taking place within the autistic personality.[8] Ten years later, she wanted to share more of her mental universe by opening 'the doors and windows' of her mind.

The title of her second book on autism – *Thinking in Pictures* – speaks to us here, although in fact Grandin devotes only five pages to her dreams. She mentions them with regard to the stairway to heaven – that is her conception of God. These dreams dated back to 1971, a period in which she developed an interest in slaughterhouses.[9] As a result of this, she went on to invent a restraint system for livestock and to become an expert on the subject.

In one of her dreams, the slaughterhouses had six storeys. Only the ground floor was designated for slaughter. A secret lift provided access to the floors above. In them had been stored a huge proportion of human culture, particularly art works and books. The dreamer walked along the vast corridors of knowledge. She realised that this library resembled life itself. You could only read one book at a time and each one brought some new knowledge. Grandin returned to that inner vision after reading some accounts of near-death experiences. People who had undergone these reported that during the experience, they had seen libraries, places in which ultimate knowledge had been deposited.

At the time of the dream, Grandin had only seen slaughterhouses from the outside. She later entered them in order to work there. One day, someone suggested that she should stun the livestock; that is, begin killing the animals. Grandin experienced the scene as if she were envisioning a dream. 'The first time I operated the equipment, it was sort of like being in a dream.' The experience of the dream was then associated with the discovery of death. 'I understood the paradox that unless there is death, we could not appreciate life.'[10] If she had not had the capacity to dream about the terrifying reality, she would not have been able to confront the idea of death.

'Some people believe that people with autism do not have emotions. I definitely do have them, but they are more like the emotions of a child than of an adult.'[11] One of the most difficult discoveries for the child to deal with is that of death. 'Perhaps because I am less emotional than other people, it is easier for me to face the idea of death. I live each day as if I will die tomorrow.'[12]

Grandin spent a long time searching for symbolic doors through which to leave a universe predominantly characterised by fear. 'In conjunction with vast amounts of stored information in my memory, the drugs have enabled me to leave the visual symbolic world behind and venture out into the so-called real world.'[13] At the time of the dream, Grandin was still trying to overcome her fear of death (the slaughter) through the mastery that would be provided by the infinite accumulation of knowledge.

VISUAL THINKING COMES TO COMPENSATE
FOR THE INADEQUACY OF THE DREAM THOUGHTS

Grandin is convinced that she is different from normal people because she thinks in images. 'Words are like a second language to me. I translate both spoken and written words into full-color movies.'[14] Grandin sets great store by this faculty for visual thinking. It has never occurred to her that this mental transformation also characterises the dream work. 'A dream-thought is unusable so long as it is expressed in an abstract form; but when once it has been transformed into pictorial language, contrasts and identifications of the kind which the dream-work requires, and which it creates if they are not already present, can be established more easily than before.'[15]

The analogy between this visual thinking and dream work does not end there. 'If I let my mind wander, the video jumps in a kind of free association ... each video memory triggers another in this associative fashion, and my daydreams may wander far from the design problem.'[16] The higher-functioning autist's daytime visual thoughts move in the opposite direction to the nocturnal visual thoughts of normal dreamers. 'Unlike those of most people, my thoughts move from video-like, specific images to generalization and concepts.'[17]

I found Grandin's account particularly moving when she described the difficulties that autists have with human relationships, including romantic relationships and sexual interactions. Like many autistic children, she was an avid viewer of the television series *Star Trek*. She identified mainly with Spock, the logical character. Normal children acquire social aptitudes 'by instinct', whereas autistic children learn social behaviour in a systematic way, in the same way that they remember what they learn at school. 'After many years I have learned – by rote – how to act in different situations. I can speed-search my CD-ROM memory of videotapes and make a decision quite quickly. Doing this visually may be easier than doing it with verbal thinking.'[18]

Grandin's description of her inner life evokes something close to the torments of hell. When she reached puberty at the age of fourteen years, the slightest tension could trigger stomach pains or panic attacks. The attacks became increasingly frequent and severe from the age of thirty years. Grandin had to have a skin cancer removed from an eyelid when she was thirty-four years old. The operation caused a terrible panic attack. She woke up in the middle of night in fear of going blind. 'To a visual thinker, blindness is a fate worse than death.'[19] It is surprising that this 'visual thinker' should not have had the oneiric images of a nightmare before she found herself waking up every night at three o'clock in the morning.

Tustin successfully treated some severe forms of autism with psychotherapy.[20] She explained that, at an early age, these children had become aware in a premature and excessively intense way of being separate from their mothers. In other words they had been traumatised before they had become able to form their psychic skin. In schematic terms, Tustin identified two principal phases in the psychotherapy of these children. During the first phase, their psychic life remains extremely impoverished. It continues to be dominated by 'object-sensations' that incorporate the mother and other people in their bodily experience.

During the second phase, the child develops the beginnings of an inner life through transitional objects that make 'self' and 'non-self' coexist, then through symbolic formations. He then relieves the inner tensions that stem from these limitations with hallucinations and, later, with dreams. Because they occur within a secure therapeutic setting, these hallucinations seem as harmless as nightmares do in normal people. They involve absent figures, sometimes family members. This constitutes an endeavour both to neutralise the pain of the absence and to accomplish an omnipotent creation in the manner of a genius telling a story.

IS DREAM LIFE PART OF PSYCHIC REALITY OR VIRTUAL REALITY?

Freud attributed to psychic reality a form of existence that was as indisputable as that of material reality. By interpreting dreams, he had invented psychoanalysis. Dreams occur in a virtual psychic space at the interface between psychic reality and shared reality. At the end of the 20th century, the concept of virtual reality posed a challenge to this rather well-worn dichotomy.

'Virtual reality is a methodology that has emerged from information technology, optics and robotics. The foray into virtual reality is a journey into an improbable region that issues from digital data stored in the computer.'[21] This virtual space seems to be well suited to an 'autistic' compartmentalisation, whereas it constantly interferes in the everyday universe. It resembles both nocturnal dreaming and diurnal reverie.

Some people prefer the term 'virtual environment' to 'virtual reality', which has gained currency. It can be defined as an environment that has been artificially created by the interaction of a human being with sensory and kinaesthetic information from a computer. We should re-emphasise the pre-eminent role played by sight within this sensory information. Sight appears to take up two thirds of the attention that we give to sensory perceptions.

Virtual reality did not invent virtual images; it borrowed them from simulation. It seems to have emerged at the end of the 1960s with the visualisation helmets that completely isolate the operator from the external world. In simulation, the operator remains outside the computer, whereas virtual reality appears to connect him directly to the computer. Keyboards, controls and levers have become obsolete. 'Virtual reality draws its force of conviction from the fact that it immerses a person in the product of his own thinking for the first time in human history.'[22] In simpler terms, virtual reality produces the conviction of being immersed in an image that is entirely artificial.

For me the term 'virtual environment' is reminiscent of the role that Winnicott attributed to the baby's maternal environment. The mother temporarily experiences a form of partial insanity (a temporary emotional psychosis) in order to respond to her baby's physical and mental needs. The mother is thus able to give the child the illusion of having created what he finds. Could she not be said to be providing him with a virtual environment? When she is a 'good enough' mother, she functions as efficiently as a computer. However, she knows how to adapt to the child's stage of growth; she progressively introduces a disillusionment that brings the environment closer to a shared reality.

THE 'CYBORG' CHILD

What is the 'cyborg child'? Major technological advances have conjured up the possibility of introducing into the human body some of the regulatory mechanisms designed for the machine in order to make it less fragile and higher-performing. Subsequently, this same neologism has been used to refer to the socio-cultural characteristics that have emerged in the generation that has been accustomed to using powerful new technologies from childhood. These apply to the sphere of information, communication and entertainment: television, computer games and the internet.[23]

From an early age, the child has equipment that enables him to connect as easily to a virtual world as to the real world. The high degree of realism attained by current simulations inevitably poses a question for mental balance: will it always be possible to differentiate virtual reality from the everyday world (in short, reality)? Synthetic images can make us believe in the real existence of human beings that have been entirely artificially created.

It is difficult to categorise technological innovations by order of magnitude. In the view of many, the introduction of the computer between the child and his environment is currently producing a similar revolution to that caused by the invention of writing. However, it is not possible to attain new achievements through the transition from one mode of communication to another without other achievements being lost in the process.

By facilitating access to virtual reality, the computer makes it possible to create non-material objects and people and to live in a place without being physically present. By using a computer, we can view, control and interact with a scene that has no material foundation. The connection with the virtual world is based on the capacity of the human brain to decode the sensory data produced by the computer.[24]

The similarity between this mode of functioning in virtual reality and 'lucid dreams' – dreams in which the dreamer is conscious of dreaming – is generally overlooked. The dreamer who finds himself in this particular state has a certain capacity to direct the course of the dream and to explore its content.

Trained subjects can indicate by various specific movements the moment at which they become aware that they are dreaming. These signals are recorded during the brain activation that is produced by paradoxical sleep. There are now established methods of enabling people to become lucid dreamers and to use this new capacity to facilitate the resolution of psychological problems.

Looking to the future, it becomes possible to envisage increasing cognitive achievements by establishing interfaces between a child's neural networks and a machine from a very early age. Access to knowledge would be amplified by equipping the child with an artificial intelligence alongside his natural intelligence.[25] This Promethean undertaking would probably alter the oneiric function. It comes as no surprise to encounter in this science-fiction fantasy a part of the universe that the psychiatrist seeks to contain and modify every day in private madness.

12
Culture Inscribes Dreams in Myths, Tales and Legends

'Should we not look for the first traces of imaginative activity as early as in childhood? The child's best-loved and most intense occupation is with his play or games. Might we not say that every child at play behaves like a creative writer, in that he creates a world of his own, or, rather, re-arranges the things of his world in a new way which pleases him? ... The creative writer does the same thing as the child at play. He creates a world of phantasy which he takes very seriously – that is, which he invests with large amounts of emotion – while separating it sharply from reality.'[1] There is no doubt that Freud's thinking had already identified a strong poetic tendency in childhood. With reference to his theory of collective psychology, Lévi-Strauss paid him this fitting tribute: 'His greatness lies partly in a gift he possesses in the highest degree: he can think the way myths do.'[2]

Freud set out to formulate not only a general psychology of the individual but also a psychology of collective life. His starting-point here was the analogy drawn by Abraham between the dream in the individual and the myth in the community. Abraham concluded that since the dream is a wish-fulfilment, the same must apply to myth.[3] This parallel remains valid for the present day, although it has to be expressed differently. Mytho-poetic thought is not the prerogative of geniuses such as Freud; it forms the basis of all well-balanced mental functioning. Myths are an essential part of life in society. Children are not directly concerned with myths, but stories and legends prepare them for these.

Roheim collected a mass of data from anthropology and psychoanalysis over several decades.[4] He developed Laistner's thesis that mythology is constituted through dreams, and nightmares in particular. The vast archive of the human imagination has seen the light of day because human beings have felt the need to tell their dreams to other people.

Why have some people told their dreams? They have needed to communicate what has been troubling them, to unburden themselves of guilt, to gain positive recognition. Dreams must have been the source material for the formation of myths. Although these elements already existed in the human unconscious, it was in dreams that they manifested themselves most clearly. Since, in these remote times, dreams were considered to be real events, they fostered the development of myths and beliefs.

Bion worked on the thesis established since Abraham's work concerning the analogy between the individual dream and the collective myth. He placed the dream and the myth in the same category: it is based on these that mental material becomes communicable and therefore analysable. In this sense, the dream, relayed by the myth, is indeed the first narrator of reality.

METAPHOR GIVES IMAGINAL FORM TO EMERGENT MEANING

Sharpe has compared the dream processes to figures of rhetoric.[5] She suggests that the composition of poems and the formation of dreams are governed by laws that originate from the same sources. The material that forms the dream narrative issues from an experience. This term refers not only to what has happened at a particular time but also to the sensations and emotions that accompanied the event.

According to Sharpe, poetic technique can be applied to dream analysis. Displacement corresponds to metonymy and condensation to metaphor. Artists seem to be capable of accessing forgotten areas of experience. They can make use of them, although they may not be aware that their knowledge of the past forms part of their creative activity. Through the associations that it generates, the dream brings the forgotten experiences and the afferent emotions into consciousness. When it is analysed, the dream reveals the unknown material that is implicitly present in the conscious mind.

The poet seeks to communicate an experience. His fundamental tools are words and combinations of sounds and images. The simplest poetic technique is known as simile. This is the connection that is explicitly made between one thing and another. The similarity emerges through a connection formed by particular words and expressions: 'like', 'such', 'as'.

The connection made by this figure of speech can be condensed by eliminating every element that formally introduces a simile. There is also metaphor, a linguistic technique that consists in using a literal term in an abstract context by analogical substitution. Metaphor is what gives rise to new senses of a word. The transition to the personal or implicit metaphor takes us to the heart of the dream narrative.

The poet often expresses that which is in some sense excluded from academic discourse. He achieves this mainly through metaphor. He enables his reader to see what is felt or to state what is seen. *If we want to describe what we have seen in a dream, we have, like the poet, to turn to metaphor.* Of course, poetry is not the only way of making this transposition, this process of transfer.

This transposition can occur in all the arts. However, poetry concerns us particularly here because a dream is first communicated through speech, before being painted, put into music, acted and so on. Metaphor establishes a close connection between that which is perceived by the senses and its meaning. It brings us very close to sensory experience, but it never eliminates the boundary that separates this experience from its meaning.

THE DREAM IS THE INTERFACE BETWEEN EMOTIONAL TRACES
AND MYTHOLOGICAL NARRATIVES

With reference to emotional nurture, Cyrulnik adopted Baudelaire's metaphor of the human brain as 'an immense and natural palimpsest'.[6] He then described it by updating the metaphor: our neural networks constantly accumulate strata of memories, each of which in turn is overlaid with forgetting.[7] Nothing that is mentalised ever completely disappears from within us. The earliest and deepest traces can always be found – at least at the time of our death. The mythological narrative is different from the trace in the palimpsest. Although it draws a similar sustenance from reality, it reconstitutes the traces through the emotions when it is addressed to an interlocutor.

I have chosen a mythological narrative to illustrate not the baby's gradual transformation into a thinking being through the maternal reverie but the completion of this transformation during adolescence, when adult sexuality is emerging. This is the Gilgamesh epic, which was written in Babylon more than thirty-five centuries ago. It tells us the story of a king with prodigious strength and greatness. He ruled over Uruk.[8] At that time, there was no clear distinction between human beings and gods. There were still several paths for moving between earth and heaven. This king was called Gilgamesh. His body was two-thirds eternal god and one-third mortal man.

At the beginning of his reign, Gilgamesh behaved like a tyrannical god. His subjects found they could no longer tolerate his conduct and they complained to the real gods. The petition was heard: the gods decided to send to earth a creature who was capable of opposing Gilgamesh. He was called Enkidu. They had instilled in him the spirit of the God of war. His violent temperament was visible in his appearance. He had long hair and his body was bristling all over with hair. His skin was almost indistinguishable from the animal furs that he wore.

As soon as Enkidu arrived on earth, he began to live among animals. No human being knew of his existence. However, one day a huntsman noticed this creature who walked just as he did but was as hirsute as the animals that he was hunting. He told his father of his discovery and was advised by him to go to the city to seek help from Gilgamesh. Immediately, Gilgamesh devised a ruse. He ordered the huntsman to take with him one of the most beautiful courtesans in the palace. When she unveiled her charms, the creature would throw himself on her, thereby setting himself apart from the herd.

At dawn, the huntsman and the servant lay in wait near the water source. When Enkidu arrived, the servant emerged from the thicket and approached him. When he saw her, he was astonished. Enkidu suddenly discovered a world of beauty and elegance of which he had never had any inkling. He felt very ashamed because he saw himself as he was. In his excitement, he overcame his unease and made love to the courtesan. The experiment was repeated on several nights. Enkidu then prepared to return to the herd. But the wild animals moved away from him. Enkidu realised that he could no longer run as he had before and that his intelligence had developed. He found that he could understand and speak the language of Uruk, having previously used the language of the animals.

Only a highly perceptive and patient observer would be able to detect the onset of thought in a baby. This extract from the myth provides us with a telescopic effect by presenting us with a similar transformation in an adolescent. If Enkidu undergoes a metamorphosis by encountering Woman, it is because she has given him, beyond the sexual relations, a capacity for reverie. She has been able to receive his primitive communication (projective identification), thus enabling him to adopt it and make it his own.

DREAM THOUGHTS AND MYTHS
INCORPORATE THE FIRST STAGE OF THOUGHT

Before embarking on psychoanalysis, Bion had studied the dynamics of small groups. He had observed that mental activities always interfered with the rational process among the participants (for example, dealing with their psychological difficulties, finding a solution to a collective problem). These activities have such emotional force that they can temporarily suspend the faculty of judgement. They reinforce the sense of vitality while blocking every development that would foster understanding.

We make use of group life to share aspects of our personality that are difficult to handle at the individual level. Each of us can thereby use defence mechanisms that would be considered as evidence of madness at the individual level. This collective regulation of mental elements that are difficult to deal with on an individual basis can lead to cultural creations such as myths, tales and legends. Oneiric thoughts and myths incorporate the first stage of thought.

According to the myth, Enkidu was immediately able to understand human language having known only animal communication. In real terms, Enkidu first established internally the capacity to transform the raw data of experience (those recorded by the animal brain). This gave him visual thinking, the capacity for psychological dreams and finally the ability to communicate through speech.

Everyday life often proves to be very different from the dramatic twists of fortune that give mythological narratives their appeal. However, I shall attempt to extrapolate from some echoes from myths or stories on the basis of some dreams that were analysed during a course of psychotherapy.

Valerie

Since her first year of primary school, Valerie had been receiving help from a speech therapist. When she had repeated her first year, she had been taken to see a psychiatrist once a week. She had come to see me when she was about ten years old for continuing difficulties at school but also for some family problems.

At our first meeting, I had been moved by her physical distress, which was accentuated by a particular affliction. She had almost emptied my box of tissues because she was constantly coughing and blowing her nose. Family life was complicated because of some reconstitutions on both the mother's and the father's side. This had caused some conflicts that were not discussed. Valerie seemed to have become the channel for these through her many symptoms. The most that she would concede was that the birth of her only sister, four years previously, had 'wrecked' everything.

By pressing her a little, I had obtained the memory of a dream. Valerie had had this at the time of her parents' separation, while she was in her first year of primary school. 'Some monsters were working with the witch. They came to get me in my bed to put me on some railway tracks. A man came to rescue me before the train arrived … It was Peter Pan. He put me back in my bed.' I asked her if she was not rather like him. She replied: 'Sometimes'. She then began to tell the dream with some mythical echoes: 'I am getting on to a horse.'

It can be difficult to decide between two possible ways of exploring the meaning of dreams: following the dreamer's associations or identifying the symbols and introducing their meanings. With Valerie, I could not easily rely on her free associations given her difficulty in mentalising. I took up the symbolism of the horse. This is one of the richest symbols.[9] Jungian psychoanalysts have seen it as the symbol of the drives in the unconscious psyche. At the threshold of puberty, galloping on a horse might represent the impetuosity of the desire that could carry Valerie away. The horse suggests the animal components that were both appealing and frightening to the blossoming adolescent girl.

It is no coincidence that Valerie dreams that her mother and stepfather are giving her a white male horse. The horse is the attribute of Apollo, the driver of the solar chariot. The horse symbolises majesty; it bears witness to the mind's dominion over the senses. But the horse easily moves from day to night, from life to death, from spirituality to sexuality. It may also be relevant that the stallion is a horse that is intended exclusively for reproduction.

We met for several months. Valerie's physical illnesses ceased almost completely. She sometimes came with her mother and sometimes with her father. We often talked about her favourite dream. She said that it was always the same, although, recording it on each occasion, I found significant variations. The most typical version would be: 'My sister is blindfolding me. My stepfather (my mother's partner) is putting me in the car. We arrive at a place where there are horses for sale. My sister opens the door. They put me on a white horse. They remove my blindfold to give me a surprise.' The dreamer was supposed not to look and to follow what was happening by listening to what was being said.

This rather idyllic version expressed the fulfilment of a conscious wish. It coexisted with all sorts of nightmares. 'I see monsters with large teeth who want to eat me. I am shouting for help but I am dying anyway. Some ravens want to eat me. (You are letting this happen?) I am fighting back with my fists. I am shouting at them: "Stop it, filthy ravens – horrible, slimy things". A vampire ghost is sucking my neck; another one is sucking at my heart. I am shouting: "help"!'

In a later version, the dream had a different ending: her mother and stepfather had already bought the horse and Valerie was climbing on to it to go back home. 'I am galloping.' A further version was supplied by a story she had read in a children's magazine. The horse was black. It was being attacked by a wolf or a puma. But this one was sad because the horse died at the end.

One day, Valerie was gloomy and preoccupied. There was some worry about her small size. 'I stopped growing when my sister was born.' She had just put on a kilogram in weight from growing 1.5 centimetres. That had not happened for a long time. A little later, she had mentioned a 'woman's secret'. She had finally confided it to me, having sworn me to silence. She was having abdominal pains. She felt as if there were a hole. She might therefore be about to start her periods. She had not talked about this to her mother. She already had some hairs on her lower abdomen. She had also lost some weight and I wondered if she might not be developing anorexia nervosa.

Her mother took her to see an endocrinologist in a university town without telling me. Nothing abnormal was found in her hormone levels. This tended to indicate a developmental arrest that was psychically determined. Valerie went into a paediatric hospital for what had appeared to be an asthma attack. She was referred to a nursing home, where she stayed for several months. When she came back, she had gone through a great many physical changes. She had grown taller and larger, but she had still not started her periods.

DREAM THOUGHTS LEAD TO MYTHICAL NARRATIVES

An emotional experience that occurs during sleep is no different in one sense from an experience during the waking state. In both cases, the perceptions connected with this experience need to be elaborated mentally before they can become dream thoughts – the first stage of thought. The first elements produced in this way can be combined in a narrative form. They pave the way for narratives with a temporal and causal structure.[10]

Some Argentinean analysts have investigated narrative deficiencies in certain patients.[11] A silent dissociation occurs that prevents coherence and correlations. They found an illustration of this mental failure in the story of *Sleeping Beauty*. Bettelheim had only addressed the problematic of puberty. However, he had anticipated the psychic theme of a dreamless sleep. 'If we do not want to change and develop, then we might as well remain in a deathlike sleep ... In such self-involvement which excludes the rest of the world there is no suffering, but also no knowledge to be gained, no feelings to be experienced.'[12] In other words, this lethargic sleep that does not give rise to connections also prevents learning from experience.

The Argentinean analysts referred only to the Brothers Grimm version, or the first part of Perrault's tale, both of which end with the arrival of Prince Charming. As in an ancient tragedy, a catastrophe is announced. The wicked fairy cries out the following curse at the cradle: 'In the fifteenth year of her age the princess shall prick herself with a spindle and shall fall down dead.'[13] No possible precaution could alter the course of destiny. On her fifteenth birthday, the young girl finds the only spindle left in the castle. She pricks her finger on it and falls into a deep sleep. The lethargy spreads throughout the whole castle; the people and animals fall into a deep sleep while thorn hedges begin to grow up all around the castle.

The twelfth and last fairy had not been able to lift the curse uttered by the wicked fairy, who was filled with destructive narcissism, having been forgotten when the invitations to the birth celebration were sent out. The good fairy could only diminish the effects of the curse: death is replaced by a deep sleep lasting a hundred years. In other terms, the young adolescent is deprived of any possibility of dreaming and constructing narratives. This suspension of mental life may appear as a protection from sexual awakening, a traumatic event in a late developing child. Narrative deficiency can be a mutilating form of defence against change.

Whereas the title emphasises the heroine's long sleep, the subtitle to some versions (in the woods) accords some importance to the protective thorns. The Brothers Grimm refer to Princess Rosamond. The rose thorns protect the princess's body and prevent her from being touched or even seen. However, their growth may also express the proliferation of a mental barrier that leaves the story in an impasse. Sometimes patients produce dream thoughts that they are unable to articulate in narrative form. Instead of developing a contact barrier between the conscious and the unconscious, they allow a defensive hedge to grow up between themselves and those around them.

13
Dreams as a Source of Literary Works

The famous writers who have reported their dreams and nightmares would make a very long list. We need only think of Swedenborg, Hawthorne, Poe, Dostoevsky and Strindberg. To these we could add the visions induced by drugs or alcohol in the works of Coleridge, De Quincey, Cocteau and Kerouac. Because I have been writing a book, it has seemed natural to give more consideration to literary creation, but we could also make connections between dreams and other forms of artistic expression. There are also the adaptations from one artistic form to another, such as Britten's skilful transformation of *The Turn of the Screw* into an opera. The nightmare, when the child manages to elaborate it mentally, can become a source of artistic creation for the adult.

READERS LIKE WHAT IS TRUE TO LIFE AS LONG AS IT IS ACCOMPANIED BY A GOOD STORY

In 1898, James published *The Turn of the Screw* to high acclaim. He was proud of his text for several reasons: first, because he had managed to write a short story 'of a perfect homogeneity';[1] second, because in this text he had achieved a fine balance between the terror that is inspired and the enigma that is subtly woven in. He had managed to revive the ghost story as a genre. He wrote this work at a time when Janet and Freud were presenting modern psychical cases with guarantees of authenticity but purged of any strange quality that might inspire a sacred terror.

The text has always defied any critic to give it a definitive meaning. It inspires doubt in the reader. Are the ghosts who seem to want to snatch the children away real, or are they only the products of the governess's morbid hysterical imagination? In so far as she is the one telling the story, this witness and observer, this narrator, could be the person responsible or even the guilty party.

The plot, which has often been discussed and adapted, runs as follows. A gentleman living in London engages an impoverished young woman from the country to look after two children. As their uncle, he has been their guardian since they were orphaned. He puts her in complete charge of their education. The heroine falls in love with him in the course of just one meeting. She travels to the isolated castle where Miles and Flora are living. The events unfold as we read her confession, written in the first person.

The young girl is then captivated by the charm of the nephew and the niece. Some doubt may be cast on their childlike innocence by a letter from the school informing them of Miles' expulsion. Very soon, two ghosts begin to feature in the life of the castle. They are identified as two people known to them who died suddenly: one of the master's servants and the previous governess, who is said to have been the servant's mistress. Convinced that these apparitions mean harm to her charges, the narrator spies on them to try to make sense of the situation. Have the children already fallen under the power of this pair of ghosts?

The way to hell turns out to be paved with good intentions. As autumn approaches, the governess puts the children in increasing danger by her very desire to save them. She reveals the presence of the former governess to the little girl. This makes her flee the estate. Left alone with the boy, the young girl clutches him to shield him from the male ghost. He dies, without the reader being able to determine whether his death has been caused by the governess's grip or by the ghost.

In the preface he wrote ten years later, James stated that he had wanted to demonstrate the power of imagination at work. While he had raced along in his invention, he had prevented his creative flow from breaching the dykes and causing a flood. The result is 'a fairy-tale pure and simple'.[2] The writer made the young girl's account lucid, although it also entails 'so many intense anomalies and obscurities'.[3] The ultimate aim is to inspire in the reader a sense of terror or horror, to give him an image of evil that he constructs entirely for himself.

As the reader may have inferred, the strange atmosphere and the plot that is both mysterious and meaningful have a dream-like quality. Edel (whose biography of James remains definitive) has explained this intuition as follows. James deliberately set out to make people (re-)live nightmares with his ghost stories. He shuffled the deck so well that every critic would in fact have explained the story on the basis of his own nightmares.[4]

Katan argued that James was driven to write his story by childhood fears of which he was then only dimly aware.[5] One day, the unexpected resurgence of these fears triggered a regressive impulse. This prompted James to find a literary form that would enable him to evacuate his own anxiety. His literary technique gave him the means of making his reader experience what had earlier frightened him.

It is well-known that making someone actively re-live something that has been experienced passively procures a sense of control. The author, who had secretly been traumatised by his childhood experience, was able to modify these repercussions by making them the basis for artistic exchange between writer and reader. Katan acknowledged that in spite of his efforts, he had not found any direct confirmation of his psychoanalytic construction in biographies of James. This does not invalidate his intuition, which I share. In fact, James began his narrative by evoking a nightmarish apparition that had terrified a child: 'an appearance, of a dreadful kind, to a little boy sleeping in the room with his mother and waking her up in the terror of it; waking her not to dissipate his dread and soothe him to sleep again, but to encounter also herself, before she had succeeded in doing so, the same sight that had shocked him'.[6]

We can imagine James as a child, deeply terrified by an oneiric vision because of having lacked access to an adequate maternal reverie. As an adult, he sought to draw his reader into the labyrinth of a nightmarish plot. He transposed his dream in order to trap the reader with a further turn of the screw. When he published the first volume of his autobiography in 1913, he reported 'the most appalling yet most admirable nightmare of my life'.[7] He indicated that he had used this as the basis for another ghost story, *The Jolly Corner*.[8]

NIGHTMARES SENSITISE THE DREAMER TO PSYCHIC REALITY

James's ghost stories bring us back to Hartmann's work. Hartmann considers that people who have nightmares are considerably more creative than others. Although this idea is far from proven, there is some evidence for it. Hartmann adduced some famous examples in support of his thesis. One of the most famous is Robert Louis Stevenson, when he was seeking to write a story about the relations between the dormant and waking parts of the self.

The writer has told how he found the inspiration for writing *The Strange Case of Dr Jekyll and Mr Hyde*. He had spent two whole days being unable to write anything. The following night, he had dreamt about two scenes: one took place at the window; in the other, a man was being pursued for a crime that he had committed. He swallowed a powder and was transformed into a monster before the eyes of his pursuers. Stevenson added: 'All the rest was made awake, and consciously.'[9]

The example of Mary Shelley writing *Frankenstein, or the Modern Prometheus* has become equally famous. But this is directly relevant to us here because it is a creative work that was produced in late adolescence. The author set out to tell a ghost story. She in fact brought about a major revival of the horror story, the Gothic novel, as a literary genre.

This is the story of a scientist who artificially constructs a man from parts of corpses. This powerful monster suffers because he inspires fear, while he feels a need for love. He finally seeks revenge by killing his creator's loved ones and then the scientist himself. This character has become something of a legend, so much so that Frankenstein's monster is often called by his creator's name.

Mary Shelley was under nineteen years old when she began to write this novel. It was published in 1818 to instant acclaim. When a new edition was published in 1831, the publisher asked the author to write an introduction explaining the genesis of the work. Shelley undertook to reply to the question that had so often been put to her: 'how I, then a young girl, came to think of and to dilate upon so very hideous an idea'.[10]

Shelley explained that she had first tried to write at a very early age. But she found it even more enjoyable to construct an imaginary universe for herself. 'My dreams were at once more fantastic and agreeable than my writings.'[11] She certainly seems to have attributed equal importance to her waking reveries and her nocturnal dreams. She nevertheless preserved a distinction between them in that what she wrote was intended for at least one other person to read, whereas she did not disclose her dreams to anyone.

During some long holidays, Mary Shelley found herself being put to the test by some adults who were more experienced writers. She wanted to write a story that would inspire deep horror. After staying up one night talking with her companions, she found herself unable to sleep. Her wild imagination began to conjure up dream images in her mind. She then saw the follower of the sacrilegious arts kneeling beside the creature that he had produced. She saw a powerful machine giving signs of life to the artificially constructed creature. She saw its maker frightened and terrorised by his own creation. Finally, the creator went to sleep. When he opened his eyes, the terrible creature was standing at his bedside.

It is no longer clear who is dreaming about whom. Confronted with the monster's 'yellow, watery, but speculative eyes', she writes: 'I opened mine in terror. The idea so possessed my mind that a thrill of fear ran through me, and I wished to exchange the ghastly image of my fancy for the realities around … I recurred to my ghost story – my tiresome, unlucky ghost story! Oh! If I could only contrive one which would frighten my reader as I myself had been frightened that night! … I have found it! What terrified me will terrify others; and I need only describe the spectre which had haunted my midnight pillow.'[12]

A CHILD'S DREAMS CAN LEAD TO REPARATION
IN AN ADULT'S ARTISTIC CREATION

It is unusual for the protagonist of an opera to be a child. However, this is the case in *L'Enfant et les sortilèges* [The boy and the magic].[13] Ravel based this two-act opera on a libretto by Colette. This opera and script occupy a position of particular importance in psychoanalysis because Melanie Klein devoted a famous article to them in 1929, in which she introduced the concept of reparation.[14]

The success of this opera has lost none of its mystery since the two artists had opposite personalities. Ravel is said never to have had a close relationship with anyone. By contrast, Colette's romantic and sexual life was both varied and well-publicised. The fact remains that their (re-)creation of a child's dream world is an almost magical success.

The plot appears to be very simple because it is about two people in a house. The interaction between a mother and her child is the source of nearly all the events that occur. The child must be about six years old, around the age at which children start primary school and learn to read and write. He is refusing to do his homework. He is arguing with his mother and flouting her. She gives him dry bread and tea without sugar. The child has a fit of rage when he is left alone. He starts to wreck the room in which he was supposed to be doing his homework. He tears his exercise books and schoolbooks to pieces. When he has finished destroying them, he shouts triumphantly that there will be no more lessons or homework and he is free and wicked.

It turns out that life cannot possibly be as simple as this for the child because he has to reckon with the sense of guilt that is projected all around him. He has had to doze off in exhaustion and he begins to dream about what is happening to him. He sees the objects that he has mistreated come to life. Everything is transformed and becomes frightening. The child is on the point of fainting and he takes refuge in the garden that surrounds the house. Large numbers of animals move towards him to attack him. An argument degenerates into a battle. A squirrel wounded by a bite falls down screeching beside the child. The child takes off his scarf and uses it to dress the animal's wounded paw.

In German, the opera has been entitled *Das Zauberwort* – 'the magic word'. The child murmurs 'Mummy' while he is tending the injured paw. He rediscovers a human world in which help can be given and in which it is possible to be good. Klein argues that the squirrel in the cage represents the penis in the mother's body. The child attacked the father's penis while it was joined with the mother's body. But he spontaneously took pity on the wounded animal. He identified with it empathetically – he felt compassion for it.

In her analyses of young children, Klein observed that unconscious phantasies arise internally at a very early stage. They influence the child's perceptions and his object relations. The child introjects both his parents' body parts and his parents joined in sexual relations. However, these internal figures are not replicas of real people. They are still imbued with the child's phantasies, emotions and feelings. A component of his inner world partly escapes the dominion of the reality principle. It emerges both in play and in dreams.

NOT EVERYONE IS BEAUTIFUL AND KIND
OUTSIDE CHILDREN'S DREAMS

The fate of Lewis Carroll's work is a surprising one: it is read mainly by adults nowadays, despite having been written for children in the 19th century. His work gives us an insight into what is left out of the picture if we restrict ourselves to a conventional view of children's dreams. I shall discuss here only *Alice in Wonderland*.[15] The heroine is supposed to be only seven and a half years old. However, it would be more appropriate to think in terms of the age that Alice Liddell was in 1862. She was around ten years old when Carroll told her the outline of this story during an outing in a boat.

During her journey, Alice discovers the world of grown-ups through the eyes of a child who is emerging from her childhood. Following the White Rabbit, Alice enters an unstable and threatening universe. All the inhabitants of Wonderland are either characters from a card game or mythical creatures (a unicorn, a griffin) or embodiments of characters from proverbs and figurative expressions.

This fantastical universe resembles the nightmare in its symbolic equations, its reversals of perspective and its substitution of common sense with nonsense. The King and Queen of Hearts reign over a court that is imbued with a perverse atmosphere. The courtiers use what resembles a form of 'doublethink' to avoid being 'vaporised' like the citizens of Oceania in Orwell's *Nineteen Eighty-Four*. The story is just coming to a close when the Queen mounts a vast trial in which almost everyone could be accused in an arbitrary way.

The King and the Queen resemble narcissistic perverts; that is, character perverts who do not seem to display any obvious sexual perversions. The King, who has jurisdiction over life and death, orders the juries to consider their verdict. The Queen protests and demands that the sentence be given first. Alice, who has started growing taller before their very eyes, criticises the Queen in a loud voice. Enraged, the Queen tells Alice to be quiet, but she refuses. The Queen gives the order to cut off her antagonist's head, but no one moves.

An accelerated growth spurt provides Alice with a reversal of perspective. She realises that she has nothing to fear from a Queen of Hearts and her court. She shouts at them: 'You're nothing but a pack of cards!'[16] At these words, all the cards fly into the air and land on top of her. Alice gives a small cry of fear. She tries to push them away with her hands. But she finds herself on a grassy bank, with her head on her sister's lap. She exclaims: 'Oh, I've had such a curious dream!'[17]

Carroll revealed to Alice that the adult world can also be frightening and perverse because the young heroine only had to open her eyes to rediscover the conventional reality of childhood. An assertion or an association that are known to be false can act as a defence against other statements that are either unknown and may be causing anxiety or are known but capable of generating an intolerable mental change.

Conclusion

There are many art works that make explicit reference to children's dreams. I shall conclude with reference to a film by two French directors, Jeunet and Carro, *The City of the Lost Children*. At the beginning of the film, the terrible Krank has been furious since he stopped having dreams (is it coincidental that *krank* means 'ill' in German?). He asks the blind people in the city to capture some children and to bring them to him on a platform on the sea. He will then be able to steal their dreams from them. But one child resists. His brother and his girlfriend try to rescue him. They then discover why the mysterious Krank needs the children's dreams so badly.

It is tempting to conclude that if children dream so much, this must be fulfilling a very useful purpose for them. However, no consensus has emerged as to the functions of paradoxical sleep and psychological dreaming. I maintain that there are multiple functions that evolve throughout the course of life. In childhood, the oneiric function influences the construction of the psyche and of the inner life, as well as its regulation. The production of dream material and the narration of oneiric experiences play a significant role in the period of life in which the emergence of sexuality brings some exposure to traumatic experiences.

'But why has evolution constructed a brain for us that periodically, during sleep, is subjected to a machinery that supplies fantastical images, paralyses our muscular tonus, suppresses most of our homeostatic regulatory functions and triggers erections?' asks Jouvet.[1]

Extensive but often contradictory knowledge concerning the 'how' of dreams has inevitably given rise to a plethora of theories as to the 'why'. Jouvet was hardly exaggerating when he made the challenging observation that: 'There are undoubtedly as many theories (or neurobiological hypotheses) of the functions of dreams as there are researchers in this field.'[2] Rather than considering all the theories, I shall limit myself to those that provide an apposite account of children's dreams.

It is essential to take account of both paradoxical sleep and psychological dreaming instead of conflating them or subordinating one to the other. There is a transition from mental images resulting from stochastic (that is, partly random) activation of the various centres in the brain to mental representations. The psychological dream only exists as an object of study when it is narrated.

It is impossible to remember, identify and select oneiric sequences without having first acquired a sense of temporal continuity in the ego and sufficient detachment to objectify that which is being related. Oneiric activity brings a reinforcement of narrative identity. Studying children's dreams has convinced me that their functions are broader than those Freud previously attributed to adult's dreams. For example, it seems more accurate to regard sleep as the guardian of the dream than the dream as the guardian of sleep.

PARADOXICAL SLEEP AND PSYCHOLOGICAL DREAMING STIMULATE MENTAL DEVELOPMENT

The functions of paradoxical sleep and psychological dreaming develop with age. Dreaming, as an attempt to fulfil an unconscious wish, proves interesting primarily at the point when the oneiric function reaches its apogee: in mid-life, which is when Freud undertook a self-analysis based on some of his dreams. If we turn to the early period of life, there seem to be several predominant functions, as described below.

• Endogenous stimulation

The less developed the brain, the greater is the proportion of seismic or paradoxical sleep. This may therefore play a role in developing the nervous system and in preparing for and establishing its activities. REM sleep would thus allow an empty repetition to occur when the sensory apparatus is disconnected. It would help or prepare the brain to react appropriately to sensory stimuli in their future complexity.[3]

If paradoxical sleep provides an important functional stimulation to the cortex during childhood, it can be hypothesised that this function continues throughout life. Jouvet took the view that this repetitive stimulation every night was designed to maintain specific connections for ensuring that fundamental instinctive behaviours are encoded. Accordingly, there is an interrelation between the genetic coding of certain specific behaviours and the events in personal history.

Jouvet then changed his view. He attributed a role to paradoxical sleep in the brain's 'iterative genetic programming'. Accordingly, the spontaneous movements observed during seismic sleep (in the foetus and the baby) signal the completion of the neurogenesis. The onset of paradoxical sleep thus corresponds to the emergence of a new mode of programming in the brain. The role of paradoxical sleep is then to maintain the psychological differences between individuals and to guarantee, at least in the human male, a certain freedom in relation to the socio-cultural environment.

• A cognitive and adaptive role

Paradoxical sleep and dreaming appear to play a part in learning, memorisation and forgetting. Waking life is not adequate to deal with the child's needs during periods of major and rapid development. Returning to processes that have been superseded but remain available confers a great deal of flexibility on mental functioning. Imaginal representation continues to occur in symbolic imitation, play and thought. Symbolic play prolongs the dream, just as the dream inspires play activity. The dream work can pave the way to resolving psychological and intellectual problems. It can lead the way towards a work of creation. It provides a form of mental 'tinkering' to complement the rational operations required by the scientific approach.

- Emotional and affective regulation

The child only accedes to the psychological dream with the aid of the 'maternal reverie', that is a form of mental metabolisation of the emotional, affective and intellectual components. We can only tolerate the affective and emotional burden imposed by external reality by behaving as if it were possible to deposit a part of our mental life with other people or in symbolic representations that are collectively deployed.

It has been argued, with good reason, that a baby could not exist without a mother's care. Similarly, the psychological dream can only develop if it is accompanied, sustained and contained by an adult psyche. The dream plays a primordial role in mentalisation and mentalisation can only occur where there is a good quality of maternal reverie.

Mentalisation is a characteristic of the human psyche since it denotes the capacity to put somatic experiences into words and images and to integrate them in such a way as to generate psychological meaning. It thus provides the foundations on which the child can think and play with mental states. This second aspect, termed the 'reflective function', corresponds to the aptitude to understand one's own and others' behaviour in terms of mental states; that is, as constituted of emotions, feelings, thoughts and motivations. This expands mental horizons by providing several perspectives on the events experienced.

- Oneiric experience has a proto-narrative potential

Ricoeur developed the theory of narrative identity.[4] I think it has interesting application to descriptions of the dream experience. The subject acquires his personal identity by re-representing to himself his experience of time in the form of a narrative. The transition from *no longer* to *not yet* would remain inconceivable if we did not perceive it as a potential story from the outset. In other words, experience has a proto-narrative potential. Our identity, our capacity to remain ourselves, is not an immutable fact but proceeds from our capacity to give it a meaning by communicating it to other people.

A story has to do more than list a series of events: it also has to organise these into a comprehensible whole. Usually, the story can be restructured based on its ending. It is often the ending that enables the story to be seen as a whole. If we do not know the ending, the plot construction can make the story intelligible; that is, communicable to an audience. The narrative is not enough in itself; its relationship with the experience that it conveys has to be put to the test.

A fundamental issue arises in the communication of the dream experience. It is a narrative identity that is played out in the plot construction and the narrative. The dreamer experiences a minor upheaval in his personal story. The dream narrative helps him to reformulate his past, his life story. As he grows up, the child finds in play and the dream narrative an inexhaustible means of honing the construction of his identity.

DOES SEXUALITY FEATURE IN CHILDREN'S DREAMS?

Sex is a major human preoccupation: as witness, the economics of prostitution, the predominance of pornography in videos, the large number of pornographic websites, the proportion of sexual crimes and offences, paedophilia and so on. In the United States, adolescents constitute only around 6% of the population but they commit 25% of the most violent crimes, including many rapes and sexual assaults. All this contrasts strangely with the near-absence of sexuality in the dream narratives published by adults.

In 1944, a German physiologist described the cycles of periodic erections in men during sleep. After the Second World War, this cycle of nocturnal erections was linked only very belatedly with the cortical activity observed during REM sleep, the period in which the most dream reports are collected after awakenings.

The external sexual organs enter a state of arousal when the man (or woman) moves into paradoxical sleep. This phenomenon is completely unknown in children. The reader may have noticed that sexuality seems to be almost entirely absent from children's dreams that are reported by adults – certainly anything that would correspond to adult genital sexuality.

This is all somewhat surprising in the light of Freud's writings on the subject. He had extended the sphere of infantile sexuality to parts of the body that are not directly connected with the sexual organs. He had also postulated that sexuality can permeate a large part of psychic life. The formulation was made possible by a clear distinction between biological sexuality and psychic sexuality.

According to Freud, infantile sexuality is present from the beginning of life. For example, erections can be observed in babies, and masturbation or masturbatory gestures in young children. There are not only early genital excitations, but also bodily zones (described as erogenous zones) with which the child seeks pleasure (sucking his thumb, holding back his faeces, for example) that are not directly associated with any biological function (feeding oneself, for example).

Freud conceded that he did not possess a universally recognised sign that would enable him to assert the sexual nature of children's activities with certainty. Does adult sexuality exist in embryonic form in the child? Or, as Laplanche argues, is the child concerned with interpreting the parents' messages, which are enigmatic because they are compromised by adult sexuality?

The problem has become further complicated because the nature of sexuality today is different from that of Freud's time. The division between the reproductive function and the pure pursuit of pleasure involving the sexual apparatus has become an even more dominant characteristic of human sexuality.

There has been a major shift in psychoanalysis during this time: the drives have gradually been replaced by object relations (love or hatred towards the breast or the mother, for instance). The emphasis has been placed on pregenital fixations; that is those that emerge before the primacy of the genital organs which allow reproduction to occur. The theory of the relational world has accorded a more important role to infant observation. The child's sexuality has thus become less apparent than in the reconstructions made by older children or adults.

THE LIMITED EXPRESSION OF SEXUALITY MAY RESULT FROM THE IMPORTANCE OF TRAUMA IN CHILDREN'S DREAMING

Children often object to nightmares being grouped together with dreams. 'Can you tell me a dream?' 'A dream or a nightmare? It's not the same thing at all!' Children report many more frightening dreams than pleasant ones. This is an indisputable fact, but their interpretation remains a matter for debate. The proportion in which these are told to adults does not necessarily correspond to what has been experienced. Are more unpleasant than pleasant dreams obtained because the latter are more easily forgotten? In other words, do happy dreams, like happy people, lack a story? A more recent hypothesis suggests that trauma occupies a prime position in the child's oneiric life.

We may wonder whether the model of the child's dream does not emerge from post-traumatic oneiric activity. The distinction between evacuative dreams and elaborative dreams reinforces the role attributed to stress and trauma in contemporary child psychiatry.

The need for an accompanying maternal reverie accredits the hypothesis of a traumatic origin to many early psychic disturbances. Wherever this reverie is deficient or absent, the baby receives the full force either of the encroaching external world or a drive upsurge. This gives rise to the hypothesis of dreaming as a possible means, if not of dissolving the impact of the trauma, at least of repairing the psychic envelope and restoring the function of the protective shield.

There is a children's story that seems to me to illustrate this viewpoint. The writer Roald Dahl created the story of the BFG, the *Big Friendly Giant*.[5] There is no one on earth who has any inkling of what he does every night. He goes all over the world whispering dreams in children's bedrooms. In the daytime, he catches dreams that float in the air like delicate soft little bubbles. He chooses the good dreams after having stored what he has caught in jars. It then only remains for him to whisper them at night in children's bedrooms with his long trumpet.

Afterword

When parents come to seek help for their child's sleep disorders, it is fairly easy to put oneself in their shoes, to imagine how their evenings are spent, to picture the possible rituals, the difficulties going to sleep or the awakening in the middle of the night. The therapist becomes attuned to a fairly conscious reality that is accessible to the senses. He may use the same words as the parents, the language of everyday life.

These same parents, regardless of their good intentions, their availability and their affection, cannot help the therapist in relation to their child's dreams. Only the person concerned can give us access to the experience of the dream. It requires an advanced level of language to tell one's dreams. The vocabulary has to describe events that are very different from those of daily life, to express impressions, emotions and feelings.

Jouvet constructed a 'dream archive' by recording his dreams over several decades. By 1978, he already had 2,525 dream memories. He wanted to create 'dream banks'. The publication of the book *La Boutique obscure* by Perec in 1973[1] encouraged him in his undertaking because the writer had composed his book with 124 of his own dreams. However, in the case of children's dream reports, these are few and far between. Most of those published are childhood dreams that have been remembered by adults.

Several developments have led to a revision of the theory of children's dreams in recent decades. It has finally become possible to study children's dreams objectively using electrophysiological recording equipment. The dream has also come to be seen as a component of cognitive development. Furthermore, in psychoanalysis, a better understanding of personality disorders other than neurosis and, above all, observation of child development have enabled us to correct a simplistic view of the beginnings of oneiric life.

To tell a dream, the child has to be able to stand back and to realise that someone exists outside of himself and that his own self (or ego) can be like another person's. This involves the capacity to separate and to mourn. The better the child can distinguish between mental representations, fantasies and external reality, the better able he is to tell his dreams.

The child needs to be helped to tolerate the frustration of weaning and to transform this and separate mentally from his mother. Winnicott coined the term 'potential space' to refer to an area of shared illusion between fantasy and reality, between the child's subjective space and that which is shared with others. This potential space first emerges between the baby and his mother. However, it is then transposed into other relationships. Ultimately, it is self-generated and it supplies the realm of art, culture and religion.

I argue that the foundation of the psychological dream in paradoxical sleep provides a model for the reflective function, mentalisation and potential space.

Dream activity provides unique but infinitely repeated instances of psychic transformation. The child can re-live the events of shared reality by searching within, integrating his emotions with his mental representations, connecting his foundational experiences with images and words and interconnecting his mental representations through symbolisation.

'The nightmare is told in order to be evacuated, like a bad internal object. It is the weed in the garden, unlike the dream that is secretly cultivated.'[2] This finely expressed observation provides a good summary of the practical approach used by paediatricians. It presents us with the widespread concept of the dream as a more or less disguised fulfilment of unconscious wishes. The dream does not need to be told; it is enough to remember it briefly before going back to sleep or getting up. Nocturnal sleep is not always the happy time that is desired before going to bed. This time needs to be idealised because of an oneiric life that is inhabited by nightmares. The latter are normal dreams. They help the child to develop and grow up if he is given some psychological support and if he is allowed to tell them. The nightmare expresses fairly directly what the child is feeling towards those close to him and his immediate circle. Having told the nightmare, the child expects to be reassured. He simply needs to rediscover the familiar images of those close to him. With these, he will be able to re-play symbolically the difficulties he is going through.

Children rarely tell their dreams spontaneously. Parents should resist their desire to know everything and combine their parental function with a therapeutic role. If an adult applies his knowledge of unconscious life, there is a risk of his convincing the child that he can understand his every thought. The child will then become worried and mistrustful. He may fear that his thoughts are being stolen or influenced. He will prefer to remain silent.

Extremes are better avoided: wanting to know the child's every thought, even the most private, or again not taking any interest in his mental life. Every child tells a dream some time. This can be a time of shared enjoyment and laughter. This can also be a wonderful time of discovery that the child is spontaneously taking his place in ancestral culture.

Unlike adults' dreams, the child's dream does not gain from being interpreted outside of psychotherapy or psychoanalysis. What is of prime importance to the therapist is the formulation; that is, the references and associations to ideas that the dream generates. The child often simply describes his dream as if it were a series of images from a film or a television drama.

Our age has been referred to as a 'visual culture'. Many children know traditional stories only from the Disney cartoons rather than from books. A cartoon artist captured this very well in a poster depicting a child with eyes that, in close-up, form the shape of a television. Information technology has further accentuated the trend and the child's pupils are also the shape of a computer screen. Oneiric life remains much richer than all the television programmes on offer to children before they go to school in the morning.

Notes

INTRODUCTION

1. De Leersnyder, H. *L' Enfant et son sommeil* [Children and their sleep]. Paris: Robert Laffont, 1998.

1. YOUNG CHILDREN'S DREAMS

1. Freud, S. *The Interpretation of Dreams. S.E.* 4–5, 1900–1901, p. 130.
2. Klein, M. The development of a child. *International Journal of Psychoanalysis*, 1923, 4: 419–474.
3. *Ibid.*, p. 461.
4. Klein, M. Narrative of a child analysis. In *The Writings of Melanie Klein, Vol. 4*, ed. R. Money-Kyrle et al. New York: Free Press, 1984 [1960].
5. Despert, J. L. Dreams in children of preschool age. *Psychoanalytic Study of the Child*, 1949, 3: 141–180.
6. The expression *sly old fox* immediately evokes the language of fairy tales.
7. Despert, Dreams in children of preschool age, p. 162.
8. *Ibid.*, p. 165.

2. PLAYING, MAYBE DREAMING

1. Winnicott, D. W. *Playing and Reality*. London: Tavistock, 1971, p. 51.

3. ADOLESCENTS AND DREAMS

1. Ladame, F. The importance of dreams and action in the adolescent process. *International Journal of Psychoanalysis*, 1995, 76: 1143–1153.
2. For a more detailed description, see Bléandonu, G. *Les Consultations thérapeutiques parents-enfants* [Therapy with parents and children]. Paris: Dunod, 1999, pp. 170–180.
3. Jeammet, P. Réalité externe et réalité interne: importance et spécificité de leur articulation à l'adolescence [External and internal reality: the importance and specifics of their interrelation in adolescence]. *Revue française de Psychanalyse*, 1980, 3–4: 481.

4. WAYS OF DREAMING IN CHILDHOOD

1. Khan, M. *The Privacy of the Self*. New York: International Universities Press, 1974.
2. Houzel, D. Rêve et psychopathologie de l'enfant [Children's dreams and psychopathology]. *Neuro-Psychiat. Enfant*, 1980, 4–5: 155.
3. Bléandonu, G. *Wilfred Bion: His Life and Works, 1897–1979*. New York: Guilford, 1994.
4. Buten, H. *When I was Five I Killed Myself*. Edinburgh: Canongate, 2001, p. 28.
5. *Ibid.*, p. 190.
6. Meltzer, D. *The Psychoanalytical Process*. London: Heinemann, 1967.
7. Grinberg, L. Dreams and acting out. *Psychoanalytic Quarterly*, 1987, 56: 155–176.
8. In Raoul Ruiz's film *The Comedy of Innocence* (2000), the young boy Camille asks his mother on his ninth birthday: 'And you, Mummy, you were there when I was born, weren't you?'

9. Segal, H. The function of dreams. In *The Work of Hanna Segal*. New York: Aronson, 1981. I am referring here only to dreams that appear to be premonitory. There is also the vast and controversial realm of the 'paranormal'. I accept that telepathic dreams can occur between people who are connected by powerful emotional bonds. There is an introduction to this in the following article by an eminent psychoanalyst: Servadio, E. 'The dynamics of so-called paranormal dreams'. In *The Dream and Human Societies*, ed. Caillois, R. & Grunebaum, G. E. von, Berkeley and Los Angeles: University of California Press, 1966, pp. 109–118.

5. DREAMS IN THE LABORATORY

1. Moore, E. B. & Fine, B. D. (eds). *Psychoanalytic Terms and Concepts*. New Haven, CT: Yale University Press, 1990, p. 57.
2. Kuhn, T. S. *The Structure of Scientific Revolutions*. Chicago, London: University of Chicago Press, 1962.
3. Foulkes, D. *Children's Dreams. Longitudinal Studies*. New York: Wiley Interscience, 1982.
4. Solms, M. *The Neuropsychology of Dreams: A Clinical-Anatomical Study*. Mahwah, New York: Lawrence Erlbaum Associates, 1997.
5. Dement, W. C. *Some Must Watch While Some Must Sleep*. San Francisco: Freeman and Company, p. 39.
6. Psychoanalysis has dispensed with explaining what it means by dream. Each individual practitioner decides with his patient what constitutes a dream narrative.
7. St. Augustine of Hippo, *The Confessions*, Book XI, Chapter 14, section 17.
8. Foulkes, D. Dream reports from different stages of sleep. *Journal of Abnormal Psychology*, 1962, 65: 14–25.
9. Foulkes, D. *The Psychology of Sleep*. New York, Charles Scribner & Sons, 1966.
10. Foulkes, *Children's Dreams*.
11. *Ibid.*, p. 8.
12. *Ibid.*, p. 301.
13. *Ibid.*, p. 293.
14. Foulkes, D. Home and laboratory dreams: four empirical studies and a conceptual reevaluation. *Sleep*, 1979, 2: 233.
15. Active or seismic sleep is a form of sleep that precedes paradoxical sleep and closely resembles it.
16. Challamel, M. J. Fonctions du sommeil paradoxal et ontogenèse [The functions of paradoxical sleep and their ontogeny]. *Neurophysiol. Clin.*, 1992, 22: 117.
17. Roffwarg, H. P., Muzio, J. N., Dement, W. C. Ontogenic development of the human sleep-dream cycle. *Science*, 1966, 152: 604–619.
18. Debru, C. *Neurophilosophie du rêve* [The neurophilosophy of dreams]. Paris: Hermann, 1990.

6. CAN BLIND CHILDREN DREAM WITHOUT THE USE OF THEIR EYES?

1. Diderot, D. Letter on the blind for the use of those who see. In *Thoughts on the Interpretation of Nature and Other Philosophical Works*, ed. D. Adams. Manchester: Clinamen Press, 1999, pp. 149–200.
2. *Ibid.*, p. 177.
3. *Ibid.*, pp. 157–158.
4. Warren, D. *Blindness and Early Childhood Development*, 2nd edition. New York: American Foundation for the Blind, 1984.
5. Manzano, J. Le développement psychosocial de l'enfant aveugle et ses troubles [Psychosocial development and disorders in blind children]. *Ann. Méd. Psychol.*, 1997, 4: 249.

6. Fraiberg, S. & Freedman, D. A. Studies in the ego development of the congenitally blind child. *Psychoanal. Study Child*, 1964, 19: 113–169.

7. *Ibid.*, p. 149.

8. Buquet, R. Le rêve et les déficients visuels [Dreaming and visual impairment]. *Psa. Univ.*, 1998, 13: 319.

9. There are two main sources of information: a study conducted in England – Burlingham, D. *Psychoanalytic Studies of the Sighted and Blind*, New York: International Universities Press, 1972 – and another that was conducted in the United States – Fraiberg, S. *Insight from the Blind*, New York: International Universities Press, 1977.

10. The traumatic neurotic aspect in the mother is explained in: Harrison Covello, A. & Lairy, G., 'Psychopathologie de l'enfant atteint de cécité ou d'amblyopie bilatérale congénitale' [Psychopathology of the child suffering from blindness or congenital bilateral amblyopie], in *Nouveau traité de psychiatrie de l'enfant et de l'adolescent* [New guide to child and adolescent psychiatry], ed. S. Lebovici, S. Diatkine, M. Soule. Paris: Presses Universitaires de France, 1985.

11. Fraiberg & Freedman, Studies in the ego development of the congenitally blind child.

12. Stern, D. *The Interpersonal World of the Infant*. New York: Basic Books, 1985, p. 51.

13. Stern, D. *Diary of a Baby*. London: Fontana, 1990, p. 7.

7. NIGHT TERRORS, SLEEPWALKING AND NIGHTMARES

1. There are two excellent books accessible to general readers that I have found useful: Challamel, M.-J. *Le Sommeil, le rêve et l'enfant* [Sleep, dreams and children]. Paris: Ramsay, 1988; De Leersnyder, H. *L'Enfant et son sommeil* [Children and their sleep]. Paris: Robert Laffont, 1998.

2. Garma, L. Aperçus sur les rêves et les activités mentales du dormeur dans la clinique du sommeil [Some insights into dreams and the sleeper's mental activities in the treatment of sleep disorders]. *Rev. franç. Psychosom.*, 1998, 14: 15.

3. Brazelton, T. B. *Your Child's Emotional and Behavioural Development*. London: Penguin, 1995, p. 189.

4. Jones, E. *On the Nightmare*. London: Hogarth, 1931.

5. Mack, J. E. *Nightmares and Human Conflict*. London: Churchill, 1970, p. 2.

6. Hartmann, H. *The Nightmare*. New York: Basic Books, 1984, p. 5.

7. I have described this little girl's treatment in an earlier work: Bléandonu, G. *Les consultations thérapeutiques parents-enfants* [Therapy with parents and children]. Paris: Dunod, 1999, pp. 94–99, 160–162.

8. POST-TRAUMATIC DREAMS

1. Celan, P. *Selected Poems*. Translated by Michael Hamburger. London: Penguin, 1996, p. 63.

2. Sadlier, K. *L'État de stress post-traumatique chez l'enfant* [Post-traumatic stress syndrome in children]. Paris: PUF, 2001.

3. Freud, S. *Beyond the Pleasure Principle*, 1920. *S.E.* 18, p. 26.

4. Ferenczi, S. The principle of relaxation and neocatharsis. *Int. J. Psychoanal.*, 1930, 11: 428–443.

5. Freud, A. & Burlingham, D. *War and Children*. New York: Medical War Books, 1943.

6. Levy, D. Psychic trauma of operations in children and a note on combat neurosis. *Am. J. Dis. Child*, 1945, 22: 7.

7. Rufo, M. et al. Rêves d'enfants au cours de la première nuit d'hospitalisation [Children's dreams during their first night in hospital]. *Neuropsychiat. Enfance*, 1980, 5–5: 199.

8. Terr, L. C. Psychic trauma in children: observations following the Chowchilla school-bus kidnapping. *Am. J. Psychiatry*, 1981, 138: 14.

9. Terr, L. C. Nightmares in children. In *Sleep and Disorders in Children*, ed. C. Guilleminault, New York: Raven Press, 1981, pp. 231–242.

10. Hartmann, E. *The Functions of Sleep*. New Haven, CT: Yale University, 1973; *The Nightmare*, New York: Basic Books, 1984; 'Outline for a theory on the nature and functions of dreaming', *Dreaming*, 2, 1996.

9. THE FORMULATION OF DREAMS AND THE DREAMER'S MENTALISATION

1. Piaget, J. Dreams. In *The Child's Conception of the World*. Translated by Joan and Andrew Tomlinson. London: Routledge, 1997 [1929], pp. 88–122.
2. *Ibid.*, p. 115.
3. *Ibid.*, p. 117.
4. *Ibid.*, p. 113.
5. Lecours, S. & Bouchard, M.-A. Dimensions of mentalisation. Levels of psychic transformation. *Int. J. Psychoanal.*, 1997, 78: 855.
6. Marty, P. *Mentalisation et psychosomatique* [Mentalisation and psychosomatics]. Paris: Les Empêcheurs de penser en rond, 1996.
7. Fonagy, P. Thinking about thinking: some clinical and theoretical considerations in the treatment of a borderline patient. *Int. J. Psychoanal.*, 1991, 72: 639.
8. Bettelheim, B. *The Empty Fortress: Infantile Autism and the Birth of the Self*. New York: Free Press; London: Collier-Macmillan, 1972.
9. Frith, U. *Autism*. Oxford: Blackwell, 1989.
10. Fonagy, P. Understanding of mental states, mother–infant interaction and the development of the self. In *Infant and Toddler Mental Health: Models of Clinical Intervention with Infants and their Families*, ed. J. M. Maldonado-Durán. Washington, DC: American Psychiatric Publishing, 2002, pp. 57–74.

10. FOETAL DREAMS

1. Stern, D. *The Interpersonal World of the Infant*. New York: Basic Books, 1985.
2. Noel, B. *Journal du regard* [Diary of the gaze]. Paris: POL, p. 24.
3. Cyrulnik, B. *Les Nourritures affectives* (Chapter 2) [Emotional nurture]. Paris: Odile Jacob, 1993.
4. *Ibid.*, p. 61, translated quotation.
5. *Ibid.*, p. 62, translated quotation.
6. Ploye, P. M. Does prenatal mental life exist? *Int. J. Psychoanal.*, 1973, 54: 241.
7. Piontelli, A. Infant observation from before birth. *Int. Rev. Psychoanal.*, 1989, 16: 413. This observational method was developed by Bick in England. The trainee analyst spends around one hour a week at the baby's home. He develops his observations with other students in a weekly seminar.
8. Fraiberg, S. *The Magic Years: Understanding and Handling the Problems of Early Childhood*. London: Methuen, 1968.
9. Stern, D. *The Diary of a Baby*. London: Fontana, 1991.
10. Emde, R., Kubicek, L. & Oppenheim, D. Imaginative reality observed during early language development. *Int. J. Psychoanal.*, 1997, 78: 115–133, p. 116.
11. Brunner, J. *Actual Minds, Possible Worlds*. Cambridge, MA: Harvard University Press, 1988.
12. Favez, N. Le développement des narrations autobiographiques chez le jeune enfant [The development of autobiographical narratives in young children]. *Devenir*, 2000, 1: 63.

11. FROM THE MENTAL IMAGE TO VISUAL THINKING

1. Freud, S. *The Ego and the Id. S.E.* 19, 1923, p. 21.
2. Lewin, B. The pictorial past. In *The Image and the Past* (Chapter 1). New York, International Universities Press, 1968.

3. Bléandonu, G. *L'analyse des rêves et le regard mental* [Dream analysis and the mental gaze]. Liège, Mardaga, 1995.
4. Eco, U. *Kant and the Platypus: Essays on Language and Cognition*. Translated by Alastair McEwen. London: Secker & Warburg, 1999.
5. Piaget, J. & Inhelder, B. *Mental Imagery in the Child: A Study of the Development of Imaginal Representation*. Translated by P. A. Chilton. London: Routledge, 1997.
6. Lévy-Bruhl, L. *Primitive Mentality*. Translated by L. A. Clare. London: Allen & Unwin, 1923.
7. Denis, M. *Les Images mentales* [Mental images]. Paris: PUF, 1979; *Image et cognition* [Images and cognition]. Paris: PUF, 1989; Lameyre, X. *L'imagerie mentale* [Mental imagery]. Paris: PUF, 1983; Tye, M. *The Imagery Debate*. Cambridge, MA: Bradford Books, 1991.
8. Grandin, T. & Scariano, M. *Emergence: Labeled Autistic*. Tunbridge Wells, UK: Costello, 1986.
9. Grandin, T. *Thinking in Pictures and Other Reports from my Life with Autism*. New York: Vintage Books, 1996.
10. *Ibid.*, p. 196.
11. *Ibid.*, p. 87.
12. *Ibid.*, p. 92.
13. *Ibid.*, p. 95.
14. *Ibid.*, p. 19.
15. Freud, S. *The Interpretation of Dreams*. *S.E.* 4–5, 1900, p. 340.
16. Grandin, T. *Thinking in Pictures*, p. 25.
17. *Ibid.*, pp. 27–28.
18. *Ibid.*, p. 138.
19. *Ibid.*, p. 113.
20. Tustin, F. *Autism and Childhood Psychosis*. London: Hogarth, 1972.
21. Jolivalt, B. *La Réalité virtuelle* [Virtual reality]. Paris: PUF ('Que sais-je?'), 1995, p. 3, translated quotation.
22. *Ibid.*, p. 5, translated quotation.
23. Lammel, A. Le cyborg child: les effets des cybertechnologies sur le développement humain [The cyborg child: the effects of cybertechnology on human development]. *Champ psychosomatique*, 2001, 22: 51.
24. Cadoz, C. *Les Réalités virtuelles* [Virtual realities]. Paris: Flammarion, 1994; Queau, P. *Le Virtuel, Vertus et vertiges* [Virtual reality: advantageous and vertiginous aspects]. Seyssel: Champ Vallon, 1986.
25. Lammel, Le cyborg child, p. 65.

12. CULTURE INSCRIBES DREAMS IN MYTHS, TALES AND LEGENDS

1. Freud, S. Creative writers and day-dreaming. *S.E.* 9, 1908, pp. 143–144.
2. Lévi-Strauss, C. *The Jealous Potter*. Translated by B. Chorier. Chicago: Chicago University Press, 1988, p. 190.
3. Abraham, K. Dreams and myths. In *Clinical Papers and Essays on Psycho-Analysis*. London: Maresfield, 1955, pp. 153–209.
4. Roheim, G. *The Gates of the Dream*. New York: Int. Univ. Press, 1952.
5. Sharpe, E. *Dream Analysis*. London: Karnac Books, 1978.
6. Baudelaire, C. *Artificial Paradises*. Translated by Stacy Diamond. New York: Citadel Press, p. 147.
7. Cyrulnik, B. *Les nourritures affectives* [Emotional nurture]. Paris: Odile Jacob, 1993 (Chapter VI).
8. This is an ancient city in present-day Iraq. *The Babylonian Gilgamesh Epic: Introduction, Critical Edition and Cuneiform Texts*, ed. A. George. Oxford: Oxford University Press, 2003; Grimal, P. *Stories from Babylon and Persia*. Translated by Barbara Whelpton. London: Burke, 1964.
9. Chevalier, J. & Gheerbrandt, A. (eds) *A Dictionary of Symbols*. Translated by John Buchanan-Brown. Oxford: Blackwell, 1994.

10. Bion, W. R. *Cogitations*. London: Karnac Books, 1992, p. 149.
11. Bianchedi, E. (ed.) *Bion Conocido/Desconocido*. Buenos Aires. Lugar Editorial, 1999.
12. Bettelheim, B. *The Uses of Enchantment. The Meaning and Importance of Fairy Tales*. London: Thames & Hudson, p. 234.
13. The Sleeping Beauty. In *Household Stories from the Collection of the Brothers Grimm*. Translated by Lucy Crane. New York: Dover Publications, 1963, p. 204; La belle au bois dormant. In *Contes de ma mère l'Oye* [Tales of Mother Goose]. Paris: Folio Junior, 1978, p. 21.

13. DREAMS AS A SOURCE OF LITERARY WORKS

1. James, H. *The Turn of the Screw and Other Stories*. Edited by T. J. Lustig. Oxford and New York: Oxford University Press, 1998, p. xlvii.
2. *Ibid.*, p. xlix.
3. *Ibid.*, p. li.
4. Edel, L. *Henry James, A Life*. London: HarperCollins, 1985.
5. Katan, M. The origin of *The Turn of the Screw. Psychoanal. Study Child*, 1966, 21: 583–635.
6. James, *The Turn of the Screw and Other Stories*, p. 115.
7. James, H. *Autobiography*. New Jersey: Princeton University Press, 1983, p. 196.
8. James, H. *The Jolly Corner and Other Tales*. Edited by Roger Gard. Harmondsworth: Penguin, 1990.
9. Stevenson, R. L. [1888] The dream origin of the tale. In *The Strange Case of Dr. Jekyll and Mr. Hyde*, ed. K. Linehan. New York: Norton, 2003, p. 91.
10. Shelley, M. *Frankenstein, or the Modern Prometheus*. In *Frankenstein by Mary Shelley, Dracula by Bram Stoker and Dr. Jekyll and Mr. Hyde by Robert Louis Stevenson*. With an introduction by Stephen King. New York and Scarborough, Ontario: Signet, New American Library. Author's introduction, p. vii.
11. *Ibid.*, p. vii.
12. *Ibid.*, p. xi.
13. Colette, S.-G. & Hoffnung, G. *The Boy and the Magic*. Translated by Christopher Fry. London: Dennis Dobson, n.d.
14. Klein, M. 1929, Infantile anxiety-situations reflected in a work of art and in the creative impulse. *Int. J. Psychoanal.*, 10: 436–443.
15. Carroll, L. *Alice in Wonderland*. Illustrated by Dudley Jarrett. London: The Readers Library Publishing Company Ltd, 1926.
16. *Ibid.*, p. 248.
17. *Ibid.*, p. 249.

CONCLUSION

1. Jouvet, M. *Le Sommeil et le Rêve* [Sleep and dreams]. Paris: Odile Jacob, 1992, pp. 210–211, translated quotation.
2. *Ibid.*, p. 57, translated quotation.
3. Roffwarg, H. P., Muzio, J. N. & Dement, W. C. Ontogenetic development of the human sleep-dream cycle. *Science*, 1966, 152: 604.
4. Ricoeur, P. *Time and Narrative*, Vols 1–3. Translated by Kathleen McLaughlin and David Pellauer. Chicago, London: University of Chicago Press, 1985.
5. Dahl, R. *The Big Friendly Giant*. Illustrated by Quentin Blake. London: Puffin, 2001.

AFTERWORD

1. Perec, G. *La Boutique obscure*. Paris: Denoël/Gonthier, 1973.
2. De Leersnyder, H. *L'Enfant et son sommeil* [Children and their sleep]. Paris: Robert Laffont, 1998, p. 169, translated quotation.

Index

Compiled by Sue Carlton